The Great
Earthquake Experiment

The Great Earthquake Experiment

Risk Communication and Public Action

Dennis S. Mileti and
Colleen Fitzpatrick

Westview Press

BOULDER · SAN FRANCISCO · OXFORD

AOL 1151-0/1

Westview Special Studies in Society, Technology, and Public Policy

Cover art courtesy of Amie Freling

This Westview softcover edition is printed on acid-free paper and bound in library-quality, coated covers that carry the highest rating of the National Association of State Textbook Administrators, in consultation with the Association of American Publishers and the Book Manufacturers' Institute.

Copyright © 1993 by Westview Press, Inc.

Published in 1993 in the United States of America by Westview Press, Inc., 5500 Central Avenue, Boulder, Colorado 80301-2877, and in the United Kingdom by Westview Press, 36 Lonsdale Road, Summertown, Oxford OX2 7EW

A CIP catalog record for this book is available from the Library of Congress.
ISBN 0-8133-8369-2

Printed and bound in the United States of America

The paper used in this publication meets the requirements
(∞) of the American National Standard for Permanence of Paper
for Printed Library Materials Z39.48-1984.

10   9   8   7   6   5   4   3   2   1

Contents

Tables and Figures

Tables

Figures

Preface

Great earthquakes have imposed incredible losses on humanity since the beginning of time, and the risk of future catastrophic quakes in the United States continues to grow. It was after the great Alaska earthquake of 1964 that the nation began to chart a course toward predicting quakes and issuing public warnings. Federal policy to achieve these ends was adopted in 1977, and the quest for the technology to predict quakes has since been earnestly pursued. The nation currently has two official governmental bodies, the National and the California Earthquake Prediction Evaluation Councils, which review quake predictions to separate predictions with and without scientific merit. The Parkfield earthquake prediction experiment began in 1985, and it is the first scientific earthquake prediction in the United States to be formally approved by both of these review councils. The prediction was followed by a comprehensive public information campaign to inform at-risk citizens.

Chapter 1 portrays the history, causes and future of large earthquakes in the United States. We trace the evolution of government policy to deal with the problems that earthquakes cause in Chapter 2. Then, in Chapter 3, we review the range of human actions that can be taken to manage or lessen quake losses. Chapter 4 presents a review of the current technology to predict quakes, traces the quake predictions that have emerged to date, and summarizes studies of societal response to those predictions. Chapter 5 reviews the Parkfield earthquake prediction experiment, which is likely the most detailed and studied prediction to emerge to date. In Chapter 6 we report on our study of public reaction to the Parkfield prediction and on lessons learned about how to make future predictions work best from a societal response viewpoint. Finally, in Chapter 7, we report on the two most recent "predictions" in the United States and how their management was impacted by lessons gained from the Parkfield earthquake prediction experiment.

The research reported in this book was supported by grant number CES-8814690 from the National Science Foundation, which is gratefully acknowledged. However, only the authors are responsible for the analyses, interpretations, and recommendations made in this work.

We also wish to acknowledge the assistance that we received from Barbara Farhar and Steven Helmericks, who worked to help us gather and sift through some of the data reported in this work. And our special thanks are extended to James Davis, the California state geologist, for being the most sociologically contaminated geologist we know, and to Sarah Nathe of the Bay Area Regional Earthquake Preparedness Project for a number of useful insights and suggestions. We are also indebted to James Goltz of the Southern California Earthquake Preparedness Project and to Paul Flores with the California Governor's Office of Emergency Services for helping us initiate our work and for making the files in their offices available for our use.

In the spirit of the interdisciplinary colleague-ship fostered by the original team that studied the 1964 "Good Friday" Alaskan earthquake and which continues in the National Earthquake Hazards Reduction Program, this book is dedicated to the earth scientists who search for reliable earthquake prediction techniques.

Dennis S. Mileti
Colleen Fitzpatrick

Large Earthquakes in the United States

Virtually every region of the United States has some sort of earthquake risk. Some areas are more vulnerable to quake damage than others because of differences in fault zone types, local geology, population densities, and local building codes and construction practices. Earthquakes in the most vulnerable areas can impose enormous losses.

The estimated cost of a repeat of the 1906 San Francisco earthquake is $100 billion. But the financial costs of great quakes pale in comparison to the possible deaths, injuries, and social disruption. For example, in 1988 the 15-second Spitak earthquake in Armenia left between 25,000 and 50,000 people dead, hundreds of thousands injured, and half a million displaced from their homes. Events as devastating as the Spitak quake are difficult for all but the most affluent societies to overcome, since they constrain productivity and the ability to achieve sustainable development.

The magnitude 7.1 Loma Prieta earthquake in the San Francisco Bay Area of California in October 1989 was less destructive than the 1988 Soviet earthquake, but it injured almost 4,000 people, destroyed 18,000 homes and 2,500 businesses, and left more than 12,000 people homeless. Its economic impacts exceeded $6 billion because of direct damage and interruptions to transportation, utilities, and communications.

The 200-year history of our nation is brief from a geological viewpoint, yet great earthquakes have occurred throughout this history. And great quakes will continue in the United States—some of them sooner rather than later.

Past Quakes

Most Americans correctly perceive that earthquakes are a problem in California. Residents of the Golden State live with a cruel irony: Much of that state's beauty and many breathtaking views owe their existence to the San Andreas fault and its mountain and basin-building activities. The fracture zone of the San Andreas runs about 700 miles from Mexico north to Cape Mendocino, where it ducks under the Pacific Ocean. This area of cities and towns is home to almost 20 million people.

Californians live with hundreds of small earthquakes on a daily basis. Most are imperceptible and go unnoticed by almost everyone except the scientists who monitor seismographic stations located throughout the state. The frequency of earthquakes in California and the rest of the nation diminishes as earthquake size increases. Although there are thousands of earthquakes in the 4.0 to 5.0 magnitude range annually, most do not produce strong ground shaking or cause much damage to human-made structures. Magnitude 5.0 to 6.0 quakes are much less frequent but often do cause damage and are widely felt. Much of the damage that results from these earthquakes is dependent on how close the quake's epicenter is to an urban area, geological conditions, and local construction practices.

> Magnitude 6 to 7 earthquakes are much less frequent but much more damaging than the 5 to 6 events. Indeed, earthquakes of 6 to 7 magnitude can be about as damaging locally, in the affected areas, as the really big ones—i.e., large or "great" earthquakes of 7.0 magnitude and higher. . . . The principal difference lies in the total amounts of energy released and hence the size of the areas affected by severe or violent shaking. Thus earthquakes of 7 to 8 and greater magnitudes may seriously affect regions 50 to 100 kilometers long (roughly 30 to 60 miles) and many kilometers wide. If their epicenters are anywhere near urbanized territory they can cause significant casualties and economic losses, and when they occur in or near large metropolitan areas, damage and casualties can be greatly increased (Bolt and Jahns 1979, pp. 2-3).

Earthquake events of great magnitude are relatively infrequent, but they do cause widespread damage and considerable societal disruption. By all scientific reckoning, a large earthquake is overdue in both northern and southern California. And a future "great" quake is expected to be more damaging than any earthquake in known history, if for no other reason than that the areas at risk have immense population densities, numbers of buildings, and economic centers.

Historical evidence clearly points to consistent and regular great earthquakes in California. The historical record goes back to about 1800, and there have been about a dozen large earthquakes in California of magnitude 7.0 or greater since then: for example, an M7.0+ on the Hayward fault in 1836 and another on the San Andreas fault in 1838, both of which affected the San Francisco Bay region; the M8.3+ quake on the San Andreas in 1857, which affected the Carrizo Plain-Ft. Tejon-Palmdale region of southern California and ruptured the fault for a distance of 250 miles; the 1868 Hayward fault M7.0+ quake in the San Francisco Bay area, which ruptured the surface of the earth from Berkeley to San Jose; the 1872 M8.3+ quake on the Sierra Nevada fault in Owens Valley; the M8.3 San Andreas rupture of 1906, which affected the San Francisco Bay region and broke the fault from San Juan Bautista to Humboldt County; the 1922 Cape Mendocino M7.5+ quake; the 1927 Point Concepcion

M7.3 quake on an offshore fault; the 1940 Imperial Valley M7.1 quake, which caused $8 million in damage; the 1952 White Wolf fault rupture of M7.2 in Kern County, which caused major damage in Bakersfield (Bolt and Jahns 1979); the 1989 Loma Prieta M7.1 quake, which affected the entire Bay region of northern California; and the M7.5 Landers earthquake of 1992 in the southern Californian desert.

The April 18, 1906, San Francisco earthquake is the best known of all Californian earthquakes. It happened in the early dawn hours, and it was the most powerful earthquake to strike that region and the contiguous continental United States thus far this century (Harris 1990). The quake was equivalent to an 8.3 magnitude, and it was felt over a 375,000 square-mile area, as far north as Oregon and as far south as Los Angeles.

> Many of the massive Romanesque buildings on the Stanford University campus disintegrated into heaps of rubble, killing two students. One hundred persons died when the poorly built Agnews Hospital for the insane almost totally collapsed. Locally along the coastline, high cliffs plummeted into the Pacific, the earth split in gaping fissures, railroad cars were thrown from their tracks, and rails were contorted into grotesque shapes. South of Santa Clara, landslides from both sides of the gulch in which the Loma Prieta sawmill was located completely buried the mill, entombing the nine men working there (Harris 1990, pp. 40-41).

Although this infamous event did directly damage structures, its secondary effects produced most of the losses and brought San Francisco to its knees. The quake burst water mains, so that fires—started by broken gas lines, overturned stoves, and severed electrical wiring—were able to spread unimpeded. The resulting conflagration raged for three days and destroyed a five square-mile section at the heart of the city (Walker 1982). An estimated 350,000 people (almost all of the city's residents) were left homeless, and around 3,000 lives were lost. These statistics were not shared with the rest of the nation for years, since San Franciscans feared that eastern bankers would become reluctant to invest in their community.

> All the downtown buildings, which had demonstrated their superior design and construction by riding out the earthquake with only minor damage, were gutted in the holocaust. More than 28,000 buildings burned to the ground. Almost no water was available to fight the fire. The quake had not only broken most of the city's water mains, it had also severed the main supply line connecting San Francisco with its reservoirs. Not until firemen, the military, and ordinary citizens impressed into service had dynamited almost the full length of Van Ness Avenue to create the most expensive firebreak in history was the fire's westward advance halted (Harris 1990, p. 42).

Great earthquakes in the United States strike in places other than California. For example, some have struck in the central United States, the Southeast, and in other western states. In fact, the largest earthquakes in our nation's history struck in central Missouri.

A swarm of earthquakes centered near the town of New Madrid, Missouri, violently shook the central Mississippi Valley beginning on December 16, 1811, and continued through the spring of 1812. This incredible earthquake activity resulted in widespread flooding as the course of the Mississippi River was changed, lakes were created, and landslides, sink-holes, and sand boils covered large areas. It is said that one especially large quake caused church bells to ring as far away as Boston. There was damage in a five-state area. The shaking from this quake was felt over a one-million-square-mile radius (Harris 1990). Fortunately, little was built then in the area of the most severe shaking; that is not the case today, however.

The nation's eastern seaboard has its own earthquake history. For example, in 1886 Charleston, South Carolina, was struck by the strongest temblor known in the southeastern United States. This M6.6 to 7.1 earthquake induced shaking intensities that ranged from IX to X on the Modified Mercalli scale (Obermeier 1986). It wrought considerable damage, completely destroyed nearly every building in Charleston, and took the lives of some 60 people. It was also felt over a wide geographic area, and minor building damage was reported from as far away as New York City and Chicago (Harris 1990).

The largest earthquake ever recorded in the United States struck on March 27, 1964. This epic geologic event was centered beneath Prince William Sound about 80 miles east of Anchorage. It shook the entire south-central coast of Alaska for more than four minutes. The earthquake released more energy than could be accurately measured on the Richter scale; subsequent estimates put it at about M9.2. Only Chile's M9.5 earthquake in 1960 exceeds it (Harris 1990).

The Good Friday quake caused massive rock slides and avalanches; collapsed roadways, bridges, and entire towns; and sent seismic waves around the world for two weeks. It raised barnacle beds and other forms of sea life 10 meters above sea level. It caused the greatest vertical displacement of the earth's surface ever measured, with about 200,000 square kilometers of the earth's crust deformed (Bolt 1978). The loss of some 115 lives in this quake was small when compared to its magnitude.

The sheer physical magnitude of the Alaska earthquake was beyond comprehension. The initial seismic waves were so powerful that they caused buildings to sway as far south as Seattle, Washington. Lengthening and weakening with distance, the radiating waves briefly lifted the ground beneath Houston, Texas, as much as four inches, and Cape Kennedy,

Florida, two and a half inches. These movements were too gentle to be felt by the residents and were only revealed by later calculations based on tide levels. And as scientists reset their instruments and watched in fascination, the waves continued to circle the globe. For two weeks the entire planet vibrated like a great silent gong. And that was just the result of the initial convulsion (Walker 1982, p. 29).

Building damage varied throughout southern Alaska and depended on the type of structure and its foundation. High-rise buildings, for example, tended to suffer more than single-story frame houses (Bolt 1978). Anchorage was hit hard by the quake.

Outside, the ground started to surge underfoot in great undulating waves, shock after shock. And as it did, Anchorage began to fall apart. Whole blocks of houses were sliding about, pavements burst open, and fissures, some up to 30 feet wide, opened and closed like yawning mouths. . . . A new six-story apartment house—mercifully unoccupied—collapsed in a heap. A crevasse gaped open beneath the Government Hill elementary school, tearing the structure down as one wing dropped 20 feet into the depression. A quarter-mile section of Fourth Avenue, the main business thoroughfare, ripped apart; bars, stores, pawnshops and cars along one side of the street dropped 11 feet in a splintered, twisted tangle of devastation. By some geologic freak the quake left the other side of the street intact (Walker 1982, p. 21).

The earthquake generated a seismic sea wave, or tsunami, that literally drowned an Aleutian fishing village—sweeping away 23 of its 76 inhabitants. The tsunami headed out to open sea and reached speeds of more than 400 miles an hour. It struck Canada's Vancouver Island, flooding Port Alberni, and then Depoe, Oregon, where it snatched four children camping on a beach. In Crescent City, California, it drowned 10 people and damaged stores in the business district. Eventually the tsunami spent itself on the coast of Japan, some 4,000 miles from its point of origin (Walker 1982).

Great earthquake events are not new to Alaska:

Between 1899, when instrumental seismic recording began, and 1961, seven Alaska earthquakes scored magnitudes of 8.0 or higher on the Richter scale. More than sixty equalled or exceeded magnitude 7.0. About seven percent of the seismic energy released annually on earth originates in the unusually active subduction zone along Alaska's coast (Harris 1990, p. 65).

The Good Friday earthquake provided scientists with the opportunity to test relatively new theories about earth mechanics and movement, it propelled earthquake research onto the national agenda, and it eventually drew political attention to the vulnerabilities of human-constructed environments.

However, the important question from a societal viewpoint is not about earthquake history; it is about future great quakes.

Future Earthquakes

Both the northern and southern parts of California are receiving a good deal of attention from earth scientists these days. Earthquake specialists agree that both parts of the state have entered into cycles of increased earthquake activity that could culminate in catastrophic earthquakes. More than California's seismic characteristics make it such a potentially destructive place—its built environment and economic networks make it one of the most geologically risky places on the face of the earth.

In human terms California is the most populous state in the U.S. and a center for many of the nation's critical technology-oriented industries. Some 10 percent of the nation's population and industrial resources are there, and 85 percent of these resources (or 8.5 percent of the nation's total) are in a strip of 21 counties along the continental margin that are well within the seismic domain of the San Andreas (Wesson and Wallace 1985, p. 35).

The potential for great earthquake activity along the San Andreas varies depending upon the segment of the fault involved. Geologists and seismologists draw on historical seismic records, paleoseismic evidence, and the research efforts of geologists and seismologists to assess seismic potential for the major segments of the San Andreas fault system in California. Based on evaluation models, which take into account the time that has elapsed since the most recent large earthquake and fault parameters such as slip rate and amount of displacement, the Working Group on California Earthquake Probabilities (1988) released probabilities for future large earthquakes in California.

In general, the probabilities for large earthquakes on both southern and northern portions of the San Andreas are considered to be high (greater than 50%) within the 30-year period from 1988 to 2018. These probabilities were raised in northern California in 1990 because of new data on past earthquakes on two Bay Area faults. Following the 1992 earthquakes in Landers and Big Bear, scientists raised the probability to 47% in 5 years for a large quake in southern California.

Many geologists and seismologists expect an 8.0+ magnitude earthquake to devastate southern California between now and certainly no later than the end of the second decade of the next century.

During the late 1970s, Kerry Sieh, a geologist at the California Institute of Technology in Pasadena, explored the sequence of major movements along the southern San Andreas fault. By digging trenches across the faultline, Sieh was able to study the number and size of fault displacements, movements that had carried rock formations on one side of the fault away from their original positions. He found that at least twelve large earthquakes had occurred during the last 2,000 years, averaging one about every 140 years. The year 1987 marked the 130th anniversary of the last great earthquake on the section of the fault, the Fort Tejon event of 1857 (Harris 1990, p. 57).

A repeat of the 1857 Fort Tejon earthquake on the southern San Andreas could cause between 3,000 and 13,000 deaths, depending on the time of day and day of the week it strikes.

The lower figure would apply if the quake occurred at 2:30 A.M. The reason emerges from worldwide observations of how earthquakes affect buildings like those in California. Briefly, the population of California is safest when it is home in bed. Wood-frame, single-family houses strongly resist structural damage by earthquakes. The higher figure would apply at 4:30 on a weekday afternoon, when much of the population is at work or on the streets. Again the reasons emerge from architecture. Old masonry buildings unreinforced by steel are likely to collapse in even a moderate quake. During the Coalinga, Calif., quake in May 1983, 30 out of 40 pre-1930 masonry buildings in the town collapsed or almost collapsed. Such buildings are common in the center of virtually all the older cities and towns in California: some 8,000 of them are in Los Angeles alone. They are gradually being replaced, particularly in Los Angeles, but significant numbers of them will remain for many years (Wesson and Wallace 1985, p. 35).

Described by some as the worst potential disaster in the United States since the Civil War (Heppenheimer 1988), an earthquake similar to the 1857 Fort Tejon quake will cause strong ground shaking for a 250-mile-long and 100-mile-wide strip of the southern San Andreas fault. The areas affected would include San Bernardino County, Riverside County, Imperial County, Los Angeles County, Orange County, San Diego County, and Ventura County. Direct and indirect economic losses are expected to total about $100 billion. Serious injuries are expected to number at least four times the number of fatalities.

The Newport-Inglewood fault, which runs between the two cities from which it gets its name, has the potential to produce an extremely destructive quake. The Newport-Inglewood fault broke in 1933 to cause the M6.3 Long Beach earthquake, which killed about 120 people.

A major Newport-Inglewood quake would be at least one and a half times as deadly as the largest anticipated San Andreas tremor. If it strikes at 2:30 a.m. . . . it will leave 4,000 dead and 18,000 needing hospitalization. . . . If it hits in late afternoon, the dead are likely to number 23,000 and the badly injured 91,000. . . . Moreover, such a Newport-Inglewood disaster would produce a total property loss of $69 billion, an estimate that could easily be on the low side. The reason is that the Newport-Inglewood cuts directly through the most populous and heavily built-up areas of the city, in contrast to the San Andreas, which runs through mountain and desert country to the north and east (Heppenheimer 1988, p. 193).

When a great quake strikes southern California, the failure of the transportation infrastructure is likely to isolate huge areas of cities for long periods of time. Disruptions in transportation, water, and energy delivery systems will be so severe that operations will not resume fully for months. In short, the entire economic and social fabric of one of the most populated areas in the United States will be torn, and repair will take great personal and societal effort and come at large expense.

The relative near-term risk for a great earthquake in northern California is almost equal to that in southern California. The resulting losses will be proportionately greater than those sustained in the area in 1906.

To begin with, let us compare the conditions of today with those of 1906. In the years since 1906, California's population has grown and spread: in the San Francisco Bay Area alone it has increased from approximately 800,000 to more than 2,000,000. Structures of new and different architectural types have been introduced into the area. There were no large facilities and essential "life lines" in 1906, such as the Golden Gate and other Bay bridges and the Bay Area rapid transit system, BART, with its tube under the Bay. We know that many deaths and injuries will surely occur. Fortunately, most Californians live in the types of wooden framed houses that have proven able to withstand earthquakes (Bolt 1978, pp. 23-24).

A repeat of the 1906 magnitude 8.3 quake will cause severe damage along the entire northern California coast. The area of destruction will range from Monterey in the south to San Jose in the east to Santa Rosa in the north. San Francisco will likely be totally cut off from ground-level communications. The collapse of the transportation infrastructure because of massive land subsidence, surface cracking, landslides, and collapsed bridges and overpasses will virtually close every arterial running north and south out of the city. San Francisco will be isolated from assistance delivered over ground (Harris 1990). Air transportation will also be severely impeded because of damage at all major airports in the area.

Perhaps the 1989 Loma Prieta earthquake has provided a foretaste of what to expect in northern California. The 1989 event was centered considerably distant from San Francisco (100 kilometers), yet it collapsed bridges, freeways, and overpasses and destroyed a portion of the Marina District—a district sitting on particularly unstable land largely made up of rubble from the 1906 quake that was used to fill in a lagoon. A similarly sized or larger quake centered closer to the densely populated portions of the Bay Area could result in significantly greater life loss, injuries, and property damage.

Much of the structural damage in the 1906 and 1989 northern California quakes was on wet, alluvial soil and landfill areas along the margins of San Francisco Bay. Almost all of the San Francisco waterfront, most areas bordering the East Bay, and the eastern part of the financial district are built on waterlogged landfill. These areas will shake intensely during a great earthquake, and the structures built on them will be extensively damaged.

> California's Seismic Safety Commission estimates that San Francisco has at least 2,000 buildings likely to collapse in a strong quake. Built of unreinforced masonry, many of these unsafe buildings are in Chinatown and south of Market Street. Most are low-rent housing. To make them quake-resistant could cost up to $30.00 per square foot, an expense owners are unlikely to undertake without raising rents and adding to the city's ever-growing crowd of homeless persons (Harris 1990, p. 51).

If the next "big" earthquake in northern California is on the Hayward fault—and this is not an unlikely scenario—Oakland, Berkeley, and other East Bay communities will suffer the most severe damage. "Many geologists believe that a 7.5 magnitude shock on the Hayward fault could claim as high or higher a toll in lives and property as a larger event on the San Andreas" (Harris 1990). A magnitude 7.5 Hayward fault quake will induce strong shaking from Petaluma and Napa south to San Jose. The greatest damage is expected in a high-risk zone from San Pablo to east San Jose. Severe damage is expected; even some well-built structures will collapse partially and numerous houses will be thrown off their foundations.

The Pacific Northwest is also vulnerable to a catastrophic earthquake. Because the quiet uplifting of the earth's surface, which accumulates strain, takes place between large earthquakes in the region, the observation of a steady rising of the Pacific Northwest coast has led some scientists to believe that this area has the possibility of large earthquakes. The area has been quiet for the past 200 to 300 years, but some think that the coastal regions of Oregon, Washington, and British Columbia could have an earthquake in the near future that could release at least ten times the energy released in the 1906 San Francisco earthquake.

> If an earthquake of that size were centered near the heavily urbanized Puget Sound region it could produce the worst natural disaster in the United States history. . . . Intense shaking will not only cause widespread sliding and ground displacement along the densely populated shores of Puget Sound, it may also trigger large waves that could sweep through city waterfronts like water sloshing out of an oversized bathtub. Damage to shipping and fuel storage facilities would be severe. Toxic spills, combined with ruptured gas mains and oil storage tanks, could produce a holocaust that both poisons the environment and incinerates crucial structures (Harris 1990, pp. 73, 77).

Although the March 27, 1964, Alaska quake claimed relatively few lives, a repeat of such an event would undoubtedly result in much greater losses due to the urbanization and population growth in the area since 1964. And Alaska's subduction zones produce, on average, a great earthquake every 50 to 100 years.

The central and eastern portions of the country share two characteristics that make them particularly prone to high losses from earthquakes. First, those portions of the country have a geology different from that in the West; seismic energy east of the Rockies diminishes less rapidly than in the West. Consequently, a quake on the continent east of the Rockies causes especially severe shaking that travels over vast distances. Second, most of the Midwest's and East's buildings were not designed or constructed to withstand even moderate earthquakes. Until recently, few people in these regions ever imagined earthquakes were anything other than a western problem.

> Some earth scientists believe that a major earthquake will strike somewhere in the eastern two thirds of the nation in the next twenty years. It is impossible to pinpoint the exact location, but the central Mississippi Valley states, South Carolina, New England and New York are among the top hazard zones. Robert I. Ketter, director of the National Center for Earthquake Engineering Research at the State University of New York at Buffalo, recently observed that a large eastern city, such as Memphis, Charleston, Boston, or New York, will probably experience a destructive earthquake by the year 2000. While the probability of a high magnitude quake hitting any particular spot is low, Dr. Ketter noted that the probability of one occurring somewhere in the eastern United States is

better than 75 to 95 percent. He warned that by the year 2010 the probability increases to almost 100 percent (Harris 1990, p. 103).

Causes of Great Earthquakes

Once thought of as constant and stable, the earth's plains, valleys, mountains, and oceans are now widely recognized to be the result of constant movements in the earth's crust. This geologic unrest exhibits itself in earthquakes, volcanoes, and other phenomena that continue to reshape most of the earth's physical features.

Scientific surveys of ocean floors, studies of fossil distribution, measurements of rock magnetism, and other observations have led to a relatively new theory—plate tectonics—that holds that the existence of mountains and the shapes of continents are visible manifestations of the inch-by-inch, centimeter-by-centimeter movement of the earth's surface layers. The millennia-long process of plate tectonics "not only pushes up mountains in crustal collisions of inconceivable force, it also creates and destroys oceans, and shatters and reshapes whole continents" (Miller 1983, p. 7).

The theory's basic premise is that the oceans and continents that compose the visible surface of the earth lie on giant crustal plates, and the plates float on molten material nearer the core of the earth. They are in a constant state of movement. Two hundred million years ago the face of the earth looked considerably different.

> The Atlantic Ocean did not exist then, and North and South America were parts of the vast landmass called Pangaea surrounded by an almost unbroken sea. Shortly after 200 million years ago, Pangaea began to break up, driven by the same subterranean forces that move the continents today. A great rift, a linear zone of deep fractures in the earth's crust, split the giant continent. As the two sides of the rift pulled away from each other, forced apart by the upwelling of molten rock from below, a large basin began to form and fill with water—the primitive Atlantic Ocean. The slow opening of the Atlantic, a few inches per year, gradually separated South America from Africa and North America from Europe (Harris 1990, p. 16).

Nowhere on earth are such shaping and reshaping movements any more evident than on the western margin of North America: "The Far West is not an original part of the continent, but consists of bits and pieces of the earth's crust that originated far from their present locations and were later grafted onto the western margin of North America" (Harris 1990). For example, most of California, the Pacific Northwest, British Columbia, and

Alaska actually originated elsewhere in the Pacific Ocean and eventually joined North America after traveling great distances in the Pacific Ocean.

> The notion that apparently solid and stable landmasses have moved vast distances around the globe, colliding and merging to create our western landscape, may seem incredible, but it is a natural consequence of the earth's plate movements. Like giant rafts, the plates carry continents, islands, and ocean basins on their backs as they travel over the hot, plastic material of the earth's mantle.
> The ocean floors, growing outward from the underwater spreading centers in the oceanic ridges have acted as conveyor belts, transporting oceanic islands and isolated microcontinents to an inevitable encounter with the leading edge of North America. Piece by piece, once autonomous landforms smashed against the granite wall of the continent, creating a coastline that is a complex accretion of exotic terrains (Harris 1990, p. 22).

Some of the most earthquake-active regions of the globe are places atop the juncture of two or more of the earth's crustal plates. One such juncture is known as the San Andreas fault, but the world has hundreds of other equally "hot" spots, for example, in Japan, Italy, Chile, the Philippines, Peru, Turkey, Mexico, and New Zealand. The Pacific plate includes the part of California that is west of the San Andreas. It is inexorably moving in a relative north-by-northwest direction along the western edge of the North American plate, which includes the balance of the continental United States. Great earthquakes are produced as these two landmasses suddenly move past each other after having been snagged and motionless for a period of time. The Cascadia volcanoes result from the melting of part of the Pacific plate as it is dragged under the North American plate.

Intraplate earthquakes, those in a land mass atop the center of a plate, are caused by other dynamics. For example, New Madrid fault zone earthquakes in the central United States and seismicity in the eastern portion of the country are not the direct consequence of plate movements. Some scientists think that they may take place on very ancient plate boundaries or seams that were once active but are no longer.

The cyclical nature of great earthquakes makes long-term forecasting of earthquake activity possible. Some geologists believe that great earthquakes happen in cycles because the crustal blocks of the earth bordering a fault zone tend to bend under strain as the blocks stick to one another. The strain mounts to the point of a sudden and cataclysmic snap—an earthquake. This buildup of strain takes place within a fairly identifiable period of time. Tracing the strain and energy release is one way in which scientists can estimate the potential for future great earthquakes. With their ability to approximate past quake events in terms of slippage, creep, and time, scientists are able to fix the statistical probability of the next great earthquake on a specific segment of a fault.

In general, the time and place of future earthquakes can be estimated by tracing the historical patterns of distance and time intervals between past earthquakes (Bolt 1978). "Seismic gaps" are areas with a high statistical likelihood for fault movement. Seismic gaps can be identified by plotting the rupture zones of past great earthquakes and then averaging the sum of slippages and displacements over a sufficiently long enough period. Thus, long-term "earthquake prediction based on what might be called a slip budget" (Wesson and Wallace 1985, p. 37) is derived. Scientific assessments about future earthquake potential are often made in this manner.

Paleoseismic research adds to the body of evidence on the cyclical nature of great earthquakes. Kerry Sieh at the California Institute of Technology developed a technique of digging trenches across a fault to see the stratigraphic record of prehistoric earthquakes. This research provides the ability to compare the cycle of prehistoric quake activity to that of recently recorded events. The intervals between ancient great earthquakes are close to the intervals observed between more recent quakes. This type of research has increased scientific confidence in the cyclical character of great quakes and has helped to validate the theory of plate tectonics.

Scientific theories and evidence speak to "objective" risk, but it is the risk people "perceive" that determines what they and society do to get ready for future disasters. Objective and perceived risk are rarely the same.

Perceiving Future Risk

Humans create their own perceptions of risk, and these may or may not match the objective risks imposed by nature and circumstance, and sometimes estimated by science.

> People perceive themselves, the world of which they are a part, and specific facts in that world; and for individuals, what is perceived is reality rather than reality itself. The perceptions which people hold, therefore, take the character of reality and serve as the basis for determining behavior, attitudes, opinions . . . and the like (Mileti 1982, p. S13).

Nowhere is the incongruity between objective and perceived risks as well illustrated as in human populations faced with potential catastrophic great earthquakes. For example, residents of California generally agree that earthquakes are a part of living in the Golden State. "Indeed, for all the dread potential, many Californians who live close to the fault look upon earthquakes as an acceptable risk in return for the Pacific Coast's salubrious climate and economic opportunity" (Walker 1982, p. 141). Most residents of the state believe in the likelihood of a severe quake at some point in the distant future, but few of them are able to accept risk in the short term—the next several years.

Unfortunately, such perceptions constrain people from taking many actions to prepare for damaging quakes. For example, very few residents of California have purchased earthquake insurance because of the perception that it will be a long time before they would ever be able to collect on such a policy. And proportionately few residents of seismically active regions of the state have done such simple things as making their houses more resistant to quake damage by bolting them to their foundations.

One of the things that enhances the perception of quake risk for the average citizen is actually living through an earthquake. Disaster experience convinces people that they are at risk to "rare" events of nature and that it is a good idea to be ready the "next time." However, escalated perceptions of risk usually wane as time passes after a quake. How the public perceives earthquake risk also constrains government actions to prepare for earthquakes.

> Because most people east of the Rockies have not felt a quake during their lifetime, they exert little pressure on public officials to improve building standards or prepare for the consequences of a major earthquake. As a result, building design and construction do not meet the earthquake-resistant standards enforced in some western states. When a large shock hits, hundreds of thousands of poorly constructed masonry buildings will collapse, many fatally injuring their inhabitants (Harris 1990, p. 103).

Severe earthquakes are generally not recognized by individual citizens as imminent risks. Of course, there are exceptions to these general rules. Some people do perceive the probabilities of future quakes more accurately than others but very few comprehend the order-of-magnitudes difference between future great quakes and those within their experience.

The social psychological process that leads people to perceive risk is more complex than what we have just described. We elaborate on that process in Chapter 6. That the public under perceives the risk of future great quakes and does relatively little to prepare places extra responsibility on governments to do things to reduce the impacts of earthquakes on citizens. The first step for a nation to begin to address any problem is through the adoption and implementation of policy. The next chapter traces the evolution of policy to reduce the problems caused by earthquakes in the United States.

2

The Evolution of
Earthquake Policy

Attempts to control the impacts of damaging earthquakes in the United States began over a century ago. The ability of buildings to withstand the impacts of earthquakes dominated the concern of some local engineers after many nineteenth-century quakes in the Bay Area. Concern became particularly acute after the 1906 San Francisco earthquake. Some engineers began to study the performance of structures during quakes and then to offer designs for new buildings that were described as "earthquake-resistant." But these practices were not widespread, and policies from governments like mandatory building codes and structural design criteria were not forthcoming.

Significant attention was not paid to earthquake losses in the United States until after 1945. World War II and postwar nuclear attack civil defense programs ultimately led to increased research into the behavior of structures under extreme conditions—nuclear blast waves and earthquakes (Olson *et al.* 1988). Studies like these were commissioned by the Atomic Energy Commission, the predecessor of the Nuclear Regulatory Commission (NRC). Performed to help cite and develop design criteria for nuclear power plants, they also created a body of physical scientists and engineers with earthquake research experience who then began to raise issues and express concerns about earthquake hazard reduction in general.

It took a major earthquake to draw national attention to the need for reducing earthquake hazards, and the 1964 Good Friday Alaska earthquake was the catalyst.

The Alaska Good Friday Quake

The Alaska earthquake caused over $311 million in property damage, in 1964 dollars, and it killed 114 residents of a relatively rural state (Olson *et al.* 1988):

Not only was the economic base of entire communities destroyed, but the resultant loss of income severely crippled the economy of the whole State and deprived Alaska of a major share of its tax base at the time when funds were most needed to aid in restoration (U.S. Geological Survey 1966, pp. 18-19).

President Lyndon B. Johnson directed the National Academy of Sciences (NAS) to conduct a comprehensive study of the earthquake. This directive began a comprehensive set of earthquake studies by numerous researchers who represented many different disciplines, including earthquake engineering and the physical and social sciences. Their work provided a comprehensive accounting of the earthquake and its effects. This was the first time in the history of the nation that a multidisciplinary approach was taken to investigate a damaging earthquake.

The research resulted in a landmark report and a call for the development of the technology needed to predict earthquakes. The report also included a proposal for a ten-year research program on prediction (Ad Hoc Panel on Earthquake Prediction 1965). The work was defined as very credible, since it had been produced by a panel of scientists from the private, university, and governmental sectors; eventually it became the foundation for the development of a national policy aimed at reducing earthquake risk.

Research recommendations were mainly related to the earth sciences—fields like geology and geophysics—and recommendations for future earthquake engineering and social science research were relatively neglected. The proposed research budget totaled $137 million; slightly over $101 million was allocated to geological and geophysical research, and the remainder was divided between earthquake engineering and other miscellaneous projects (Ad Hoc Panel on Earthquake Prediction 1965). The geographical focus for the recommended research was Alaska and California-Nevada; quake risk in the rest of the nation was ignored.

The 1965 panel and report motivated considerable action in some federal agencies. In 1966 another ad hoc committee was convened, chaired by the Director of the U.S. Geological Survey (USGS), which consisted solely of members representing different federal agencies. This committee issued its report in 1967, and it called for a ten-year earthquake hazard reduction program that would involve a partnership between science and society.

The 1966 panel proposed a substantially larger budget ($220 million) than the budget recommended by the 1965 panel. Most notably, it broadened the scope of earthquake threat: "All areas of the United States experience earthquakes at some time and no area should be considered as free of potential earthquake hazard" (Ad Hoc Interagency Working Group for Earthquake Research 1967, p. a). Additionally, the 1966 panel provided long-term earthquake forecasts and loss estimates. The panel stated that "many moderate, a few severe, and probably one great earthquake can be expected within the United States between now and the year 2000. Billions of dollars in damage may be expected and loss of life may be hundreds to thousands" (p. b).

The 1966 panel called for more than earth science research, and it also pointed to the national need to engage in earthquake engineering research in order to learn of ways to mitigate earthquake hazards in the United States. The report also took pains to note the psychological, sociological, and economic problems with implementing an earthquake prediction system. At the very least, the 1966 report "set a pattern for organizing interagency program plans, defined an agenda of policy issues, clarified the national threat and broadened program emphasis from prediction research to hazards reduction" (Olson *et al.* 1988, p. 148).

The 1964 Good Friday Alaska earthquake provided the impetus for the nation to clarify the issues involved in earthquake hazard reduction and to define future research needs. But the promulgation of a national earthquake hazard reduction policy still required someone or something outside of federal agencies to help it along. The applied engineering and seismological research communities outside of government provided this contribution.

The National Academy of Engineering (NAE) convened its own committee on earthquake engineering in 1969 to develop an earthquake program plan and to establish specific future research priorities. Seismologists also began laying their proposed research agenda on the table at about the same time. The National Academy of Sciences, through its National Research Council (NRC), also put forth its thoughts about a national earthquake program.

The NAE's Committee on Earthquake Engineering report (National Academy of Engineering 1969) demonstrated that earthquake-related research needs consisted of various intertwined disciplines including earthquake science, engineering, and socioeconomic and policy concerns. It provided links between earth science as a "pure" science and engineering as "applied" science. The first chapter in the report, "Socioeconomic Aspects of Earthquakes," drew specific attention to the implications of earthquakes for society and also raised important policy issues.

The report by the National Research Council's Committee on Seismology (National Research Council 1969a) voiced considerable concern that the field of seismology was losing the momentum it had built up during the years immediately following World War II. The report called for new programs emphasizing earthquake prediction research.

The National Academy of Sciences 1969 report (National Research Council 1969b) not only summarized lessons learned from the Alaskan earthquake but also focused attention on actions that could promote hazard reduction programs. However, it recognized that much of the responsibility for implementing hazard reduction activities was in the hands of state and local governments. One of its implementation recommendations was that a task force in the Office of Science and Technology "be established to recommend a comprehensive government program directed toward reduction of losses from hazards such as earthquakes" (National Research Council 1969b, p. 11). The recommendations were not limited to earthquakes because the committee viewed earthquakes as a Californian and Alaskan problem, and "Congress [could] not be expected to reflect a continuing national concern for the earthquake hazard" (National Research Council 1969b, p. 11).

In essence, the final recommendations provided by the varied committees that investigated the Alaska earthquake redirected earthquakes from a national issue back to a local-regional concern. Nevertheless, "events would soon alter the situation, and key actors would come to the fore to carry the concept of a Federal earthquake program from discussion to policy" (Olson *et al.* 1988, p. 16).

The San Fernando Quake

The 1971 San Fernando earthquake shook the entire Los Angeles area and caused over $500 million in losses. The earthquake helped to move national policy along the path toward a national earthquake hazards reduction program. This quake was the first significantly damaging event in a large metropolitan area since the Alaska earthquake, and it led immediately to congressional hearings. Senator Alan Cranston, then a junior U.S. senator from California, became the champion of a national earthquake policy.

The initial bills introduced by Senator Cranston expanded the nation's support for earthquake prediction research. However, as his bills failed during the following several years, Senator Cranston and others began to broaden the scope of the bills introduced. "From 1971 to 1977 earthquake engineering research was added, an interagency management/coordination structure was proposed, social science research was recognized, and other elements were included in drafts and actual bills—all building incrementally toward 1977 legislation" (Olson *et al.* 1988, p. 17).

A second major influence began in 1972 when the Federal Office of Emergency Preparedness (OEP) office in California initiated activities on earthquake preparedness. The Region 7 OEP recognized that a public law would be required to get OEP's national office involved in federal hazard reduction policy. Consequently, the Congressional Disaster Relief Act of 1970 (P.L. 91-606) was interpreted by the OEP to require "that a full and complete investigation and study be conducted to determine what additional improvements could be made to prevent or minimize the lóss of life and property due to major disasters" (Office of Emergency Preparedness 1972, p. 1).

The congressional report that resulted provided a vehicle for potential political support. It was multihazard in focus and included earthquakes as one of the 10 hazards reviewed. Most significantly, the report was prepared by an agency with a "mission" rather than by one with a vested interest in scientific or engineering research. Additionally, as a staff agency within the executive office of the president, the OEP was able to garner top-level support for its mission, and "President Nixon, in his 1972 State of the Union Address, referred to accelerating the application of science and technology to reduce the loss of life and property from natural disasters" (Olson *et al.* 1988, p. 20).

The Chinese Prediction and the Palmdale Bulge

In 1975 and 1976 critical events mobilized Congress to enact a national earthquake hazard reduction policy. A successful earthquake prediction by the Chinese in 1975 reportedly reduced casualties to almost zero as thousands of residents of the city of Haicheng were evacuated hours before a 7.3 magnitude quake destroyed most of the city's buildings (Mileti, Hutton, and Sorensen 1981). Other extremely damaging earthquakes in China, Guatemala, and other countries led the USGS to remark that 1976 could be "the worst year of this century for deaths due to earthquakes" (U.S. Geological Survey 1976, p. 8).

In 1976 the USGS reported that it had discovered an "uplift of the earth's crust along a section of the San Andreas fault [the "Palmdale Bulge"] that had been relatively quiet since the great earthquake in 1857, [representing] cause for concern" (U.S. Geological Survey 1976, p. 8). The USGS noted that the uplift might or might not be a precursor to an earthquake but that the observed uplift was like those observed before other earthquakes, for example, the 1964 quake in Niigata, Japan (Mileti, Hutton, and Sorensen 1981). Furthermore, "the perception that Russian and Japanese prediction technologies were more advanced and better financed than the U.S.'s" (Olson *et al.* 1988, p. 21) added to the political salience of predicting earthquakes and the earthquake hazard at the national level. Additionally, Senator Cranston had achieved seniority in the Senate about this time, and this enabled him to further his federal earthquake policy cause:

Cranston recruited Representative George Brown to join him. Brown was a respected member of the House Science and Technology Committee from the earthquake-prone San Bernardino-Riverside, California area.

And he had the support of Charles Mosher (R. from Ohio), a ranking minority member of the Committee. Representative Mosher had a special interest in science and technology issues. Their combined ability to secure coauthors and gather votes was enhanced by recent information that all 50 states were vulnerable to earthquakes, and 39 were subject to "major or moderate seismic risk" (Olson *et al.* 1988, p. 25).

Enactment and Implementation of the Earthquake Hazard Reduction Act of 1977

The important congressional pieces were now in place. Earthquake hazard management came to be viewed as a needed and viable strategy for reducing earthquake risk. Earthquake risk came to be viewed as a national problem requiring the concerted attention of a wide variety of agencies and legislators. The one remaining piece necessary for bringing a national policy to fulfillment was support from the executive branch of government, the office of the president.

The President's Commission on Science and Technology was formed early in President Ford's administration. The purpose of this commission was to study the relationship between science, technology, and public policy. The commission ultimately provided the president with a list of 25 major science and technology initiatives and specifically suggested that earthquake hazard reduction was an area that could greatly benefit from increased attention. Additionally, the Ford administration saw the Palmdale Bulge in California as an important political issue that needed a visible and immediate response. "The response took two forms: (1) transferring money from NSF to USGS and (2) forming the Advisory Group on earthquake prediction and hazard mitigation" (the "Newmark-Stever" panel) (Olson *et al.* 1988, p. 26).

In 1976 the Newmark-Stever panel was charged to develop an expanded research program for the USGS and the National Science Foundation (NSF). This panel produced a report that had a major policy impact and addressed earthquake prediction and hazard mitigation through a direct focus on USGS and NSF program activities (U.S. Geological Survey 1976).

After more than a decade of earthquake experience, technical recommendations, and constituency-building the legislation was on the brink of passage as the 94th Congress and the Ford administration ended. However, one major change remained before the threshold would be crossed: inauguration of President Carter (Olson *et al.* 1988, p. 28).

The Carter administration embraced the proposed legislation for a national earthquake program, but it did ask that the proposed National Advisory Committee, an Earthquake Hazards Reduction Committee, and the Office of Earthquake Hazards Reduction be removed from the bill. The administration proposed that a comprehensive implementation plan be developed before organizational arrangements were considered, and it recommended that the program contain a continuing research program. The administration's recommendations were incorporated into the act, and the assignment of agencies responsible for carrying out the act was left to the discretion of the executive branch. Fourteen years after the Good Friday earthquake, after more than a decade of recommendations and reports, and after five years of legislative effort, the president signed on October 7, 1977, the first and only major national earthquake policy legislation in the United States—the Earthquake Hazard Reduction Act of 1977 (P.L. 95-124).

The act required the president, within 30 days of signing the legislation, to appoint the agency that would be responsible for preparing the implementation plan, and the implementation plan was to be submitted to Congress within 210 days of enactment. The budget for the implementation plan involved year-by-year targets through 1980. No lead agency was formally named in the implementation plan, but budget authorization did designate the U.S. Geological Survey and the National Science Foundation as the agencies that would receive funding for implementation activities.

President Carter requested that an implementation plan for the act be prepared by the Office of Science and Technology Policy (OSTP). The plan (Working Group on Earthquake Hazards Reduction 1978) represented the culmination of efforts to bring the earthquake community together to define future needed work. The plan purposefully neglected budget concerns and the question of which agency would assume primary responsibility for implementing the act. The report consisted of a list of recommendations that included preparedness and response planning, earthquake prediction and warning, earthquake hazards reduction construction programs, land use planning, and communication and education (Working Group on Earthquake Hazards Reduction 1978). President Carter sent the plan, The National Earthquake Hazards Reduction Program (NEHRP) (Executive Office of the President 1978), to Congress. The plan briefly stated the goals of the act, the general intent of the program, and the responsibilities of the involved federal agencies for meeting the act's objectives.

Although the plan talked about the importance of program leadership and referred repeatedly to the "lead agency," it was silent about which one would lead. Whereas specific agencies were designated as responsible for the implementation of other items, this section called for action by the as-yet undesignated "lead agency." Presumably, it was known that the lead agency would be the FEMA, since reference was made to the "President's Reorganization Project" (PRP), which led to the creation of the FEMA (Olson *et al.* 1988, p. 38).

The enactment of the National Earthquake Hazards Reduction Act set the stage to stimulate ways to deal with the earthquake problem in the country, and to attempt to induce the earthquake-endangered public and local governments to practice earthquake preparedness and hazards mitigation. Ideally, the result would be a decrease in losses from future damaging earthquakes:

> The Earthquake Hazards Reduction Act of 1977 established the National Earthquake Hazards Reduction Program (NEHRP). The overall goals of this program are to reduce future losses of life and property from earthquakes, and to mitigate the severe socioeconomic disruption that could be induced by a catastrophic earthquake. A range of federal agencies participate in this program, and each works toward the accomplishment of one or a mix of principal NEHRP activities. These include hazard delineation and assessment, seismic design and engineering research, preparedness planning, and earthquake hazard public awareness. Basic research is funded by the National Science Foundation (NSF); however, it is the U.S. Geological Survey (USGS) that holds program and operational responsibility to conduct research that could lead to earthquake predictions and warnings (Mileti and Sorensen 1990, pp. 1-3).

Achieving goals like these required translation of the act's broad objectives into specific agency and program operations. Although the act did not specify a lead agency, it was strongly implied during debate that the Federal Emergency Management Agency (FEMA) would take the lead when it was formed. The program essentially remained without a formal leader until FEMA was created in 1979. Informal leadership was provided in the interim by the other federal agencies named to participate in implementing the act. These were the U.S. Geological Survey, the National Science Foundation, and the National Bureau of Standards (NBS), which is now the National Institute of Standards and Technology (NIST). The missions of these federal agencies, along with that of FEMA, constitute the current effort to implement earthquake hazards reduction activities in the nation today.

The early years of the USGS were primarily focused on the economic aspects of geology, for example, exploration for minerals, petroleum, and groundwater. But in recent years geologic hazards such as landslides, earthquakes, and volcanoes have received increasingly more of its research attention. The Alaska earthquake of 1964 heightened the USGS earthquake research focus, and the results of the Alaska Earthquake Panel's report led to the formal organization in 1966 of the USGS National Center for Earthquake Research in Menlo Park, California. The current role of the USGS in the National Earthquake Hazards Reduction Program involves a wide range of disciplines and does work to reduce earthquake risks throughout the United States. The USGS program places high priority on four geographical regions in the United States—southern California, the San Francisco Bay Area, the Pacific Northwest, and the central United States—and it is divided into four basic elements.

First, the program is developing a better understanding of the source of earthquakes. This research element seeks to further knowledge about how and why earthquake faulting occurs. Research includes field, laboratory, and theoretical studies that are specifically directed toward earthquake source processes. The second program element studies potential for earthquakes in different regions of the country. The work defines and characterizes earthquake sources, determines rates of seismic activity, and pinpoints where different areas are in their overall earthquake cycles. This element of the program houses earthquake prediction research. The third element of the USGS program, earthquake effects, documents and estimates future ground shaking, ground failure, and damage to structures, property, and loss of life. The fourth program element is aimed at enhancing the application and use of research results from the prior three portions of the program. For example, research findings must be presented in a format available and accessible to engineers, governments, and the general public. Work in this program component is designed to stimulate the public and private sectors to take specific actions that will reduce the losses from future quakes.

The National Science Foundation provides a vital link between the federal government and university communities. The NSF does not itself conduct research, but it does decide to whom—largely university-based researchers—federal research funds will be granted. NSF-sponsored research provides information to a wide array of users nationwide. Much of NSF's earthquake-related research in the past decade or so can be directly attributed to its role in NEHRP.

NSF contributed to the creation of the National Center for Earthquake Engineering Research (NCEER) at the State University of New York (SUNY) in Buffalo. NSF also sponsors construction materials research to investigate substances that fare well under earthquake stresses. NSF supports research on innovative engineering techniques that will lead to structural systems that will resist earthquakes.

NSF's earthquake engineering program also includes research into the behavior of lifelines during strong ground motion, and the means for strengthening such systems. The lessons learned from the 1971 San

Fernando earthquake, 1985 Mexico City earthquake, and 1986 El Salvador earthquake illustrate the value of this research program and the need for discovering ways to protect lifeline systems from the effects of earthquakes.

In addition, NSF sponsors quick-response research immediately following moderate and major earthquakes in order to gather perishable data before they decay. This quick-response research obtains data that would otherwise be lost.

NSF research activity investigates the political, economic, and sociological factors that influence the use of earthquake hazards reduction measures. Although societal research on earthquakes has been sponsored by the NSF for decades, it has never had the same strong resource support as other research areas, for example, engineering. This may be because there are relatively few social science researchers active in the earthquake field. Moreover, only in recent years have social issues related to the implementation of mitigation actions for earthquake hazards become apparent. Another factor in the relatively weak support for social science research may be the national tradition of emphasizing technical solutions to problems. Yet

> another reason can be traced back to a social science grant that caused NSF some problems in the late-1970s. The notoriety about alleged financial mismanagement created a political liability that bedeviled the NSF earthquake program for several years, especially just as the social science element was establishing its own identity. The issue attracted an unusually high degree of press attention. In response, the House Appropriations Subcommittee for the NSF, chaired by Congressman Boland from western Massachusetts, drastically cut the money for the social science element. . . . One result was that money for social science research declined so that almost nothing was available for several years, discouraging new people from entering the field just as it was starting to develop (Olson *et al.* 1988, pp. 49-50).

The National Institute of Standards and Technology is charged under the NEHRP to address safe and economical new construction and the assessment and upgrading, retrofitting or demolishing of existing hazardous buildings. The primary aim of the NIST's laboratory research program is to develop an understanding of advanced design criteria for improving seismic behavior of new or existing structures. The intent of this objective is to provide sound information to those who make decisions regarding building codes and standards and to make sound recommendations about the repair and retrofit of existing structures (Federal Emergency Management Agency 1987).

The Federal Emergency Management Agency provides the prime leadership and coordination role for all NEHRP activities. Additionally, FEMA actively participates in implementation activities; for example, it currently shares sponsorship with the Governor's Office of Emergency Services of the Southern California Earthquake Preparedness Project (SCEPP) and the Bay Area Regional Earthquake Preparedness Project (BAREPP) in northern California. These projects and others like them in other parts of the nation are aimed at developing the interest of local governments, the private sector, and the public in planning, mitigating, and preparing for earthquakes.

The role of FEMA in the National Earthquake Hazards Reduction Program is large not only because it plays the program's lead role but also because it is oriented to foster action at the local level. FEMA prepares an annual budget for the program, seeks to ensure implementation of earthquake hazards reduction measures throughout the United States, prepares NEHRP plans and biennial reports for submission to Congress for review, provides grants and technical assistance to states, prepares and executes a comprehensive education and public awareness program, prepares and disseminates information on building codes and practices, and provides emergency response recommendations to local communities.

The National Earthquake Hazards Reduction Act was amended in 1980, three years after it was enacted, and became P.L. 96-472. The most marked accomplishment of these amendments was to name the FEMA as the lead agency responsible for the act's continued implementation. The amendments also called for a five-year plan and the creation of the National Earthquake Prediction Evaluation Council (NEPEC)—a group of expert earth scientists and seismologists who are to evaluate the scientific credibility of earthquake predictions.

Almost all of the 1980 amendments reflected operational concerns about making the NEHRP more action-oriented rather than reflected shifts in the actual policy. For example, some of the amendments required annual reports, a model planning project in the form of the Southern California Earthquake Preparedness Project, and a requirement that the formal issuance of any earthquake prediction be the responsibility of the director of the U.S. Geological Survey.

The National Earthquake Hazards Reduction Program has most recently been amended in the NEHRP Reauthorization Act of 1990 (P.L. 101-614). Some of the provisions of that act include the establishment of the advisory committee for the program that was removed from the original act by the Carter administration, housing for postearthquake investigations in the USGS, and a significant increase in funding for program activities. The 1990 amendment to the act also updated the goals and objectives of NEHRP to include, for example, educating society about the threat of earthquakes and the means available to address the risks, developing model building codes and practices for quake hazards reduction, improving application of research results, and developing a mechanism for ensuring the availability of affordable earthquake insurance.

The nation has come a long way since the Good Friday earthquake of 1964 in recognizing its earthquake problems, in adopting adequate national policy to address those problems, and in funding earthquake-relevant research and applications. In the long run, the purpose of these activities is to enhance the adoption and application of a range of activities in the nation to reduce what is lost when earthquakes strike, and to be better able to respond to the residual losses.

3

Actions That Reduce
Earthquake Risk

The National Earthquake Hazards Reduction Program provides the nation with a federal policy and action context for taking steps to reduce losses from future earthquakes. The specific actions available to implement the program are varied, and each of them attacks earthquake problems in different ways. Each of these actions is available for use, in varying degrees, by different groups, for example, individuals, families, governments (local, state, and federal), and small and large businesses in the private sector. These hazards reduction tools include land use planning, building codes and construction practices, insurance, emergency planning and response, planning for disaster recovery, and reconstruction and earthquake prediction and warning. Each of those tools is continuously fine-tuned as new knowledge is discovered that makes it more effective (Tobin *et al*. 1992). This chapter reviews these "adjustments" to the earthquake hazard.

Land Use Planning

Land use planning based on geologic conditions and earthquake-shaking potential can help to reduce losses of life and limb, as well as losses to the built environment (Joint Committee on Seismic Safety 1974). Land use planning seeks to determine the type, amount, location, and character of private and public development in areas subject to damage from shaking during future quakes. In general, land use planning

> deals with the comprehensive arrangement of land uses so as to produce a functioning urban environment which is responsive to the full range of economic, social, political and physical factors. . . . When considering hazard mitigation with respect to any parcel of land, a planner might consider a variety of mitigation measures: increased structural safety, increased land stability, change proposals for future land use, change [in] occupancy standards and change [in] existing land use. The ultimate objective is to minimize the exposure of persons and property to risk, but in a manner consistent with other community needs (Mader 1980, p. 176).

Land use planning involves such societal issues as acceptable risk and the social benefits to be derived by the uninhibited use of the land as a resource. Land use planning to reduce the risk from earthquake is not performed in isolation from other land use concerns. Ideally, planning would assist in developing ways to promote socially desirable management and uses of land in concert with a specific community's risk to a specific earthquake hazard. Throughout the nation, however, this practice is currently underutilized as a means to deal with earthquake problems; the extent of its use in different areas of the country is contingent on local differences in quake risk, hazards, and cost/benefit concerns. There is a growing realization that a good proportion of the reconstruction costs after an earthquake must be met by government programs, which translates into the use of tax dollars (Bolt 1978).

Effective land use planning demands that attention be given to a community's preevent earthquake vulnerability. In fact, "planning" implies that the future holds risks and that efforts to reduce those risks are important. Therefore, a primary basis for developing sound earthquake hazard reduction strategies is assessments of seismic risk zones, estimates of likely future shaking intensities, and associated degrees of ground and soil transformation.

Geological studies assess such things as historical seismicity and fault activity in an area, soil conditions, landslide potential, and land transformation such as subsidence and liquefaction. Such factors can be considered by being incorporated into seismic zoning maps. Such maps typically depict the relative or probabilistic nature of earthquake activity in a specified area.

> Most maps of relative risk mark zones with an arbitrary numerical or alphabetic scale. . . . Maps of probabilistic risk give an idea of the underlying statistical uncertainty as is done in calculating insurance risk. These maps give the odds at which a specified earthquake intensity would be exceeded at a site of interest within a given time span (typically 50 to 100 years) (Bolt 1978, p. 174).

While land use planning efforts may ideally take place before an earthquake, they are typically at the heart of the debate as communities begin reconstruction after a damaging earthquake. The majority of postearthquake efforts are aimed at restoring the community to its predisaster economic and social levels. The recovery period is not always the best time to develop conscientious and rationally based land use plans, especially since competing economic interests and citizen anxiety about restoring things to normal can quickly constrain the process (Mader, Spangle, and Blair 1980). Typically, it takes an earthquake disaster to prompt policymakers to develop and adopt land use regulations. As a result, planning decisions and community participation in the process are often wrought with emotional overtones as competing interests seek to have their needs met at a time that society is intensely disrupted and inclined to restore normalcy as quickly as possible. Furthermore, changes in land use policies are influenced by a number of factors, for example, community size, existing land use patterns, economic bases and stability, the varied social and cultural characteristics of the community, and especially involvement by government outside the affected area.

In a series of case studies on earthquakes, Mader, Spangle, and Blair (1980) found that federal government actions had a major impact on determining local land use decisions for earthquake hazards reduction. Federal redevelopment and reconstruction funds historically have influenced land use changes.

> Essentially, it was found that land use changes are made when the costs are borne primarily by the federal government, especially through redevelopment projects. However, federal procedures and regulations pose problems in using land use change to reduce future risk (Mader, Spangle, and Blair 1980, p. iv).

These problems generally involve issues concerning authorization and funding of redevelopment projects, questions about funding sources, problems with appropriate guidelines to determine property values, and difficulties with administering disaster assistance programs that often lead to conflict between federal and local government.

The circumstances following the 1964 Alaskan Good Friday earthquake demonstrate how this process operates. And the process hasn't changed much over time. Seismically induced landslides were responsible for a large proportion of the damage that the Good Friday quake caused in Anchorage and its environs. The small town of Seward was severely damaged by landslides due to seismic sea waves, and the town of Valdez was especially damaged: "during the earthquake a large submarine slide and slide-induced waves destroyed Valdez' port facilities and much of its commercial area" (Mader, Spangle, and Blair 1980, p. 6).

The federal government assumed the primary responsibility for reconstruction after the quake. President Johnson appointed the Federal Reconstruction and Development Planning Commission to coordinate reconstruction efforts and planning for long-term economic recovery. Nine task forces were created within this commission, one of which was the Scientific and Engineering Task Force, responsible for addressing many land use planning issues. This task force produced a series of maps depicting areas in which federal funds could not be used for reconstruction unless special construction criteria were met (Mader, Spangle, and Blair 1980).

The majority of actions taken to reduce future quake risk following the earthquake were those that the federal government funded. As a result, the town of Valdez was literally relocated inland about two miles, and Seward's dock facilities were relocated, leaving its major waterfront area vacant. The primary land use activity consisted of turning major slide areas in Anchorage into recreation parks. The land use changes that were made "were accomplished through publicly-funded redevelopment projects; changes were not made through conventional rezoning or other land use controls" (Mader, Spangle, and Blair 1980, p. 7). And pressures to rebuild quickly after the earthquake led to ignored concerns about especially hazardous land zones, particularly in privately owned areas and in the absence of legislated land use restrictions.

While land use planning can be an effective way to reduce seismic hazards, reducing earthquake risk also often demands knowledge about design characteristics and construction practices for buildings. In this sense, land use planning and "seismic risk maps are usually translated into building codes" (Bolt 1978, p. 176).

Building Codes

Building codes and practices provide a means to populate hazardous areas with structures more resistant to damage. Such codes reduce earthquake hazards through the adoption of technological construction practices backed up by government sanctions.

> Historically, ordinary market forces have not always provided acceptable levels of fire and seismic safety, structural integrity, or sanitation in the nation's housing and building stock. Hence, society has intervened through its police power to impose certain standards on the marketplace in the interest of public safety and welfare. Local building regulation is based on exercise of this police power. Therefore, most building codes and other regulations containing earthquake resistant requirements are intended to protect life, and only circumstantially to reduce (not eliminate) property damage (Federal Emergency Management Agency 1985, p. 12).

Such an intervention strategy generally "involves some kind of recognition of basic physical systems, of the living part of the community which is related to those systems, and of the constraints imposed by materials and interactive processes upon the kinds of action which may be taken" (White and Haas 1975, p. 202). Although it is not yet possible to build "earthquake-proof" structures, "most buildings could be designed and constructed to resist significant structural damage, and the possibility of total collapse" (Ayre, Mileti, and Trainer 1975, p. xv).

Earthquake engineers, through the use of computer-simulated analyses of building motions and data from actual earthquakes, have developed sophisticated structural design and building materials to resist failure during major earthquakes. Engineering research on the design of earth-quake-resilient structures and mapping research on seismic zones over the past couple of decades have provided useful information to those responsible for developing building codes. However, research on seismic engineering has mostly focused on large structures such as high-rise buildings, dams, and nuclear power plants; lesser structures such as low-rise buildings, as well as interior nonstructural characteristics of buildings and building materials, have received less research attention (Ayre, Mileti, and Trainer 1975; Bolt 1978). As a result, building codes are more frequently developed and adopted for larger structures, and private dwellings are often ignored.

Building codes can also be used to address the repair and retrofit of existing structures. Such attention is warranted, since it is reasonable to expect that buildings built prior to earthquake-resistant codes have a considerably higher risk of damage in an earthquake than those built to newer codes. Building codes for existing structures, however, have a special set of problems:

> Old buildings probably present the most difficult problem of all. They may be lucrative rental property or tax write-off for the owners, homes and community foci for a great number of persons who cannot or will not live anywhere else, and may also be potential death traps due to the danger of collapse or fire. The two general classes of problems concern the physical condition of the structures and the social and economic constraints on doing anything about the conditions (Ayre, Mileti, and Trainer 1975, p. xvii).

Defining the extent of this problem is not easy. For example, "the number of unreinforced masonry buildings in the city of Los Angeles is about 8,000. The total, when other classes of potentially hazardous buildings are added, however, remains unknown although obviously much greater" (Federal Emergency Management Agency 1985, p. 10).

The Federal Emergency Management Agency considers the following types of buildings especially hazardous in a major earthquake anywhere in the United States (Federal Emergency Management Agency 1985, pp. 11-12):

- concrete frame buildings without special reinforcing;
- precast concrete buildings, including pre-1973 tilt-up structures and more recent tilt-up and precast composite buildings;

- "soft-story" buildings (those with the lower story lacking adequate strength or toughness);
- buildings with prestressed concrete elements and/or posttensioned concrete slabs;
- steel frame or concrete frame buildings with unreinforced masonry walls;
- reinforced concrete wall buildings with no special detailing or reinforcement;
- unreinforced masonry-wall buildings with wood or precast concrete floors;
- theaters and auditoriums having long-span roof structures;
- large, nonengineered wood-frame buildings;
- buildings with inadequately anchored exterior cladding and glazing; and
- buildings with poorly anchored parapets and appendages.

Earthquake-resistant building codes began to appear in some cities of California as early as 1933 (Ayre, Mileti, and Trainer 1975). And like many policy efforts, earthquake-resistant building practices have often been initiated and adopted in reaction to a damaging earthquake.

On Friday, March 10, 1933, at 5:54 p.m., southern California was shaken by a magnitude 6.3 earthquake on the Newport-Inglewood fault. The city of Long Beach was severely affected by the quake. The total number of buildings destroyed in this seismic event is unknown; many public school buildings sustained serious structural damage, and several were completely destroyed. "Investigations of the damaged school buildings indicated that building designs had not, in most cases, included provisions to resist seismic forces; and even where included, were inadequate as many school structures failed to resist forces imposed by ground movement" (Mann 1979, p. 9). Several pieces of legislation grew out of the failure and collapse of school buildings in the Long Beach earthquake.

The California legislature immediately appointed a committee to review the state's school structure safety program. The committee prepared Assembly Bill 2342, which "passed the Assembly the day it was introduced, passed the Senate a few days later and was signed into law by Governor Rolph exactly one month later, on April 10, 1933" (Mann 1979, pp. 9-10). The commission was headed by Assemblyman C. Don Field, and the resulting piece of legislation became known as the Field Act. The original legislation stated that much of the damage from the Long Beach earthquake could have been avoided if buildings and other structures had been constructed to meet earthquake-resistance standards. The act specifically mandated that the earthquake-resistant design of newly constructed or reconstructed buildings replace' public school buildings damaged or destroyed by the earthquake. The principal objectives of the Field Act were "to ensure that public schools and community colleges in California are constructed to resist, insofar as practical, forces generated by earthquakes, gravity, and wind" (California Seismic Safety Commission 1991, p. 125).

The authority provided the state by the Field Act applied primarily to newly constructed public school buildings and was not retroactive. Nor did it provide the state authority to condemn or close any public school building (Mann 1979). By the middle to late 1930s, legislators observed that the intent of the act was not being fulfilled. Thus, in 1939 the legislature enacted the Garrison Act, which applied to pre-Field Act school buildings. The Garrison Act required that a school board take corrective measures if school buildings under its domain were unsafe. However, the act provided that if it failed to become law members of the school board could not be personally held responsible for any damage or injuries caused by the unsafe buildings during an earthquake. Then

> in 1963, the provisions which specifically absolved the board members of personal liability were repealed. In 1967, the Garrison Act was amended by the Greene Act to require examination by January 1, 1970, of all school buildings not constructed under the Field Act, and provided immunity for school board members upon initiating action to examine such buildings. In 1968, the act was amended to require abandonment of un-safe school buildings by June 30, 1975. In 1974, the act was amended to allow the use of unsafe buildings until June 30, 1977, if rehabilitation processes had started by June 30, 1975. The State Allocation Board granted an extension allowing use beyond June 30, 1975 (Mann 1979, p. 18).

In 1943, the Field Act was broadened to include all lower education facilities (kindergarten through community college) throughout the state. State-owned institutions of higher learning (universities) and private schools still are not governed by this statute.

The 1933 Field Act and subsequent amendments are not the only pieces of legislation aimed at building construction to reduce earthquake losses in California. The Seismic Structural Safety of Hospitals program was enacted in 1972 in response to the collapse of several hospitals during the 1971 San Fernando earthquake. This program seeks to ensure that new hospitals or additions to existing ones are able to resist the forces generated by earthquakes, gravity, and wind. The Hospital Construction Monitoring and Structural and Architectural Review program was enacted in 1983; the objectives of this program are to ensure that all state-licensed health facilities are constructed to meet earthquake safety standards.

The 1985 Essential Services Buildings program is intended to see that state-owned or state-leased essential services buildings are also designed and constructed to be seismically resistant. An unreinforced masonry building program was also enacted in 1985; the objectives of this program are to motivate city and county departments of building to identify potentially hazardous unreinforced masonry buildings and to establish programs to mitigate hazardous conditions.

Shortly after the 1989 Loma Prieta earthquake, which destroyed or damaged several highway structures in the San Francisco Bay Area, an Earthquake Research and Development Plan was enacted by the California legislature. The objectives of this plan are to research and develop methods, techniques, and technologies for the identification, analysis, and seismic retrofit of existing potentially hazardous buildings and facilities. The plan is also meant to help develop and prepare building standards and administrative regulations relating to the seismic retrofit of existing buildings.

The state of California continues to view the building of structures in quake-resistant ways as a prime device to reduce its vulnerability to future earthquakes. "Future initiatives are planned that address both the public and private sectors and include regulations to encourage hazard reduction in new and existing vulnerable facilities" (California Seismic Safety Commission 1991, pp. 1-2).

Insurance

Earthquake insurance is another disaster adjustment strategy. Insurance, however, is somewhat different from land use management and building codes and practices. It provides a means for distributing the cost of individual reconstruction across the larger population to avoid bankruptcy, rebuilding loans, and other public assistance. Insurance could also presumably act as a disincentive, discouraging people from occupying areas vulnerable to natural disasters (White and Haas 1975).

> Insurance can serve two important functions in mitigating the consequences of natural hazards. If rates reflect the risk of living in a particular area, insurance can exercise guidance over the extent to which hazard-prone areas are developed. Secondly, following a disaster such coverage provides a means of recovery for damaged homes and businesses. Without insurance, victims may be forced to rely on federal disaster relief, conventional bank loans, or declare bankruptcy (Kunreuther 1978, p. 23).

Earthquake insurance might also act as an agent of change in terms of indirectly encouraging other preparedness and mitigation activities such as anchoring houses, bolting water heaters, and doing other things to reduce damage during future earthquakes.

American insurance companies began offering earthquake coverage in 1916, but few policies were sold in that year even in California, despite the fact that it had been only 10 years since the great 1906 San Francisco earthquake. This might be explained by the perception that the most significant damage from that earthquake was caused by fire and that regular fire protection would suffice.

Insurance companies also saw fire as the primary agent of loss in the 1906 quake and as a result they offered low rates, created small company reserves, and bought little if any reinsurance. Fortunately for the insurance companies, the low number of policies written spared them high losses in the ensuing years, especially after the 1925 Santa Barbara earthquake. Earthquake insurance purchases began to rise steadily following the Santa Barbara quake. This trend has continued with the exception of the depression and World War II periods (Kunreuther 1978).

> Earthquake insurance practices differ slightly between the Pacific Coast states and the remainder of the United States. In the west earthquake insurance usually is written as an endorsement to the standard comprehensive homeowners policy and is subject to a minimum deductible of 5, 10, or 15 percent, depending on the type of construction. . . . Rates are a function of the risk zone in which the structure is located and its type of construction. For California there are three different hazard zones and eight types of construction, ranging from frame dwellings (the most stable) to buildings with clay, tile, unreinforced hollow concrete block, or adobe walls (the most vulnerable) (Kunreuther 1978, p. 39).

Few people purchase earthquake insurance even though it is a sensible investment (Kunreuther 1978; Palm 1981; Palm 1990). A possible explanation for this arises from how people tend to perceive risk, which in turn influences their decisions about what actions to take. Earthquakes are generally perceived to be low-probability events and something that will happen in the distant future. Future damaging earthquakes are simply not usually viewed as events that will affect the people who consider them. Therefore, insurance is simply viewed as not cost-effective.

An alternative to people singularly developing perceptions of risk that directly lead to insurance purchase behaviors is found in incentives for purchasing insurance. The paucity of incentives for purchasing insurance may also help explain the phenomenon of few insurance purchases relative to earthquake risk. Mortgage lenders, for example, typically do not require buyers of homes located in known fault zones to purchase quake insurance despite the likelihood that extensive earthquake damage to an uninsured home may result in defaults on loan payments and possible bankruptcy (Palm 1990). Earthquake insurance is generally not "part of the fire and extended coverage policy that is generally required as a condition for a mortgage. . . . Earthquake insurance policies are underwritten entirely by private firms and normally are sold as an endorsement on a fire and extended coverage policy" (Kunreuther 1978, p. 23).

Although the federal government flood insurance program subsidizes as much as 90% of an individual policy and provides a reinsurance fund for the insurance companies to guard against bankruptcy after a major disaster, a federally subsidized earthquake insurance program is not yet available. However, congressional hearings began shortly after the 1989 Loma Prieta earthquake on earthquake hazard mitigation and earthquake insurance. The federal government is now seriously considering the development of a nationally subsidized earthquake program (House Committee on Banking, Finance and Urban Affairs 1990).

The governor of California took steps to initiate a state earthquake insurance program shortly after the Loma Prieta quake, largely in response to difficulties in financing housing reconstruction. The state enacted the California Residential Earthquake Recovery Fund in 1991 as a stopgap insurance program. The objectives of this program are to provide property owners with a limited amount of low-cost residential earthquake damage insurance coverage to supplement the deductible on their standard insurance or earthquake insurance policies. The program provides participants initial funding up to $15,000 for damage repairs to single-family residential properties. It will eventually establish a residential retrofit loan program to mitigate potential seismic hazards when the insurance fund reaches $1.5 billion (California Seismic Safety Commission 1991).

Insurance programs provide a tool to mitigate losses before an earthquake event by setting aside the financial resources needed for restoring the human-built environment. Activities such as land use planning, development of building codes, and insurance programs represent efforts to make rebuilding the damaged environment less stressful and more effective and efficient. However, reconstruction and restoration does not follow immediately after a disaster strikes; the immediate aftermath of a damaging earthquake focuses on emergency response and relief.

Emergency Planning and Disaster Relief

Emergency response takes place in the immediate aftermath of an earthquake disaster. It typically lasts for several days to about a week. The emergency actions undertaken are varied and include efforts to locate and rescue victims and to provide food, water, clothing, shelter, and medical care to those who need it. This work is performed in an effort to deliver emergency services and to stop loss and disruption as soon as possible.

Emergency response and the provision of immediate relief after a major disaster is performed by numerous government and private agencies across national, state, and local boundaries. However, initial emergency response is more likely than not performed by surviving disaster victims themselves. Adequate planning for emergency response and disaster relief is prudent, since it facilitates the overall community response effort.

An example of what can go wrong when preevent planning is not in place is provided by the response and relief effort that followed the 1988 Spitak earthquake in Soviet Armenia. Planning for earthquake disaster response and the provision of relief was virtually missing at all levels of government in the Soviet Union. Instead, there was a general reliance on the normal centralized bureaucratic order to provide emergency response and relief during disaster. However, the people of Soviet Armenia became double victims: victims of the earthquake disaster itself, as well as victims of a highly structured centralized bureaucracy.

> They witnessed the lack of an initial bureaucratic response to the cataclysmic disaster. Indeed, the earthquake did destroy the bureaucratic order found in modern society where people do not do things, but rather bureaucracies do. For example, bureaucracies supply water, food, housing, work, electricity, education; bureaucracies rescue people, offer medical aid, treat the injured; and these things are usually coordinated through a system we know as government. The earthquake changed all that; bureaucracies were themselves earthquake victims, other bureaucracies took a while to converge on the scene, and when they finally did appear they hardly functioned as a coordinated network (Earthquake Engineering Research Institute 1989, p. 152).

The expectation that bureaucracies can be relied upon to tend to the immediate relief needs of a disaster-stricken community may very well be unrealistic. It was certainly unrealistic in the Armenia earthquake disaster.

> What emerged in the period before traditional response bureaucracies could arrive was a decentralized set of grassroots bureaucracies or work groups comprised of surviving victims. People organized themselves into

groups to do the work (search and rescue) that needed to get done. In fact, rough estimates are that 95% of the people who were rescued were rescued by other victims. Converging international and national search and rescue teams, once they arrived, were able to rescue only another 5% (Earthquake Engineering Research Institute 1989, p. 153).

As with many prior disasters, the disrupted society reorganized itself immediately following the earthquake. Survivors instantly took steps to fill the void left by traditional emergency response organizations. However, this responsive social reorganization lacked coordination among groups, and the spontaneously organized workers lacked sufficient knowledge and means to get the job done effectively and efficiently. Incredible amounts of international aid and assistance also arrived—supplies and search-and-rescue teams converged on the stricken area.

Although such altruistic world response is appreciated and has come to be expected, the lack of coordination and planning presented serious problems during the relief period. For example, many donated items were of little or no use during the emergency period. The convergence created airport congestion and traffic problems, and people who might otherwise have been put to more useful tasks were needed to process the donated items.

Survivor relocation became another major problem, creating a type of disaster itself. The bureaucratic efficiency of these efforts may have added to this problem. It is estimated that approximately a half-million people were relocated within just a couple weeks of the earthquake. Some people went to friends and relatives and some were relocated in resort hotels provided by the central government, and many children were sent to a hospital in Yerevan.

[Relocation] occurred so quickly and efficiently that it became impossible to keep track of who went where. . . . Many families sought to adopt orphans but the children could not be put up for adoption because no one knew if they were in fact orphans or if unidentified relatives had been relocated (Earthquake Engineering Research Institute, 1989, p. 154).

Planning for the emergent grassroots response organizations would make them more effective following disaster. For example, viewing the public as a resource rather than as a problem could lead to programs to train the public in effective response techniques. Training communities in search and rescue, in first aid, and in effective organization skills would undoubtedly increase the response effectiveness of inevitable emergent grassroots work groups. In fact, within just a year or so following the

Loma Prieta earthquake, the city of Oakland began a program to organize and train neighborhood groups in emergency response techniques.

Perhaps even the best disaster planning can never fully prepare a community to provide effective and efficient emergency response and relief after a great earthquake. However, experiences with past disasters provide valuable lessons on what to expect and how to plan for a more effective response to future disasters.

Disaster Reconstruction

The most lengthy and costly stage of disaster recovery is reconstruction. Reconstruction involves the fixing or replacing of destroyed and damaged structures and economies and other social activities. The hope is that communities will approach functional levels equivalent to or better than those in the predisaster period. Reconstruction sometimes can involve the actual physical relocation of a town, but this alternative is almost never chosen.

> Cities and towns are almost never relocated. Planners are apt to look at a damaged, debris-ridden city and say, "Let's leave all this and start all over at a safer site." The idea of starting from scratch with a chance to "do it right" is inherently appealing to planners. However, experience teaches that relocation almost never happens for several reasons: (1) safer sites are hard to find nearby, (2) substantial infrastructure is still intact or repairable, (3) the cost to relocate is usually higher than the cost to rebuild, and (4) people have strong associations with "place" even in economic systems without private land ownership (Spangle and Associates 1991, p. 3).

During reconstruction a community's capital stock is rebuilt to predisaster levels and usually in the same geographic location as before the disaster. Sometimes this also involves the redevelopment or creation of structures and land areas for commemorative purposes.

> The indicators of the end of the period are the replacement of the population and of the functioning equivalent of their needs in homes, jobs, capital stock and urban activities. . . . Certain aspects of reconstruction may go on long after the period is over, centered around the construction of large-scale projects. . . . Commemorative, betterment and developmental reconstruction projects serve three varied but sometimes interrelated functions: to memorialize or commemorate the disaster; to mark the city's post-disaster betterment or improvement; or to serve its future growth or development. Characteristically such projects are large, and usually financed by the government. The activity may extend over twice the

period required for replacement reconstruction (Kates and Pijawka 1977, p. 3).

Reconstruction following any disaster, especially after a major earthquake, is a long and involved process: "The shape and appearance of the rebuilt city concerns everybody. Exciting visions of a newly designed city compete with strong desires to restore the city exactly as it was before disaster struck" (Spangle and Associates 1991, p. 3). Such concerns often generate intense community debate. In addition, earthquakes create severe housing problems, exacerbate existing housing problems, and can actually cause business patterns to shift.

Public facilities are usually rebuilt very quickly, especially facilities providing essential lifeline services. Rapid restoration of transportation, communication, and utility systems becomes a very high priority, since an intact infrastructure is necessary if any sense of a normal life is to be achieved.

Economic conditions of a community prior to an earthquake affect the speed and progress of recovery and reconstruction. Economically sound communities are in positions to recover in an efficient and effective manner; communities struggling with economic survival prior to the disaster struggle with it even more afterward. "Land ownership is also a critical factor. Property owners resist changes they think will reduce the value of their property or the profitability of businesses. They make critical investment decisions which can govern the nature and pace of rebuilding" (Spangle and Associates 1991, p. 5).

Ironically, major earthquakes can provide opportunities to make a city safer in future seismic events. For example, cities can be rebuilt to be safer and urban areas can be redesigned to be more pleasing and conducive to business.

This reconstruction process often takes years. For example, reconstruction efforts following the Loma Prieta earthquake are still ongoing more than three years later and will be so for several years to come. This lengthy process is especially visible in Santa Cruz, California. Santa Cruz is the largest city close to the Loma Prieta earthquake epicenter, and it was extensively damaged. The housing stock throughout much of Santa Cruz County was severely damaged. Many homes were completely destroyed. Nearly the entire business area of downtown Santa Cruz was destroyed either during the earthquake or from demolition afterward. In Santa Cruz's downtown shopping mall alone, 24 of its 45 unreinforced masonry buildings were lost. "Earthquake damage was heavy to homes in the sparsely populated region of the Santa Cruz Mountains near the earthquake's epicenter. Here ground shaking was particularly violent [and] the future safety of homesites in the mountains is uncertain, complicating decisions about rebuilding" (Spangle and Associates 1991, p. 66). And even though special mapping of seismic risk in this mountainous area was almost immediately undertaken, much controversy about safety remains and continues to impede reconstruction decisions.

Limited business activities in Santa Cruz were resumed within a matter of a few weeks after the earthquake; much of this business has been conducted in temporary bubble-tent facilities. Full reconstruction in Santa Cruz is many years away. The future shape and character of the city and its surrounding community continue to remain a matter of imagination and speculation.

Prediction and Warning

Prediction and warning systems bear an interesting relationship to other hazards management tools like land use and building codes. They are the last lines of defense available to protect the public after other ways to deal with earthquake risk have reduced it to some acceptable level. However, prediction and warning systems for infrequent events may not make economic sense. Warnings are cost effective only when a risk becomes a looming actual event and when having an inadequate system or no warning system at all is politically and socially unacceptable.

The goal of any prediction and warning system is to notify the public of potential disaster in the hopes that the information will be used by those who receive it to protect themselves. Warning systems typically cut across a variety of organizations. This obvious goal is too often lost sight of as people focus on their narrow duties in a warning system. For example, earthquake-detecting organizations monitor the natural environment in order to warn political jurisdictions of an impending hazard. People in such organizations may view the passing of warning information on to a governor as the end of their warning responsibility. A state bureaucracy that passes the information along to local government may view its warning role as completed when local officials are informed.

The organizational and bureaucratic structures of society in the United States are such that the general goal of setting up a warning system—to provide citizens at risk with information to maximize the odds that they will engage in some appropriate response to the risk—is often left for someone else to attain. Moreover, the warning information needed by the public is broader than that needed by organizations. Consequently, public warnings are often inadequate.

Several specific goals apply to any warning system. The first is to get people at risk to listen to emergency information and to prepare them to respond with some sort of protective action. The second is to guide people to take what is considered to be the best protective action. The third is to help people understand that their actions are part of an organized response to protect the community.

People respond to predictions and warnings in a number of ways. One is to go about planned normal activities. The second is to seek more information. The third is to take some form of protective action. These alternatives are not mutually exclusive. People frequently take all of these actions in response to hearing a prediction or a warning.

The protective actions that can be performed in response to a warning can be divided into three categories: One can seek protection in an appropriate shelter, for example, stay home in one's single-story wood-frame house after an earthquake warning; second, one can move away from the area of likely impact, for example, evacuate; and third, one can do things that block or divert impacts, for example, strap a water heater, bolt heavy furniture to walls, and remove objects that could fall from shelves and cabinets. All of these actions are rational and would undoubtedly result in lower casualties following the predicted event. Nevertheless, there are a variety of myths about public response to warnings. Unfortunately, these myths are prevalent in American society and they often impede government and public decision-making in warning circumstances.

Among the most pernicious fallacies are the following. First, the public simply does not panic in response to warnings of impending disasters. Hollywood and Tokyo screenplays are probable culprits in the propagation of the panic myth. Research documents that people panic only in situations in which there is closed physical space, in which there is an immediate and clear threat of almost certain death, and in which escape routes will not accommodate all those in danger in the minutes before death comes to those left behind.

Second, the public rarely if ever gets too much information in an official warning. It is true that people do not remember all the information contained in a warning if they hear it only once. But detailed and frequently repeated warnings can overcome this. Emergency warnings are simply not subject to the 30-second rule of Madison Avenue attempts to sell toothpaste and deodorant soap. People are information-hungry in a warning situation and should, therefore, be provided with all the information they need. Such information can easily be made part of warning messages and bulletins.

Third, the effectiveness of the public's responses to warnings is not diminished by what has become known as the "cry wolf" syndrome if they have been informed of the reasons for previous "misses." Obviously, there would be a negative effect on subsequent public response if there were frequent false alarms and no attempts made to explain why there were false alarms, and if the cost of response was high. Yet, false alarms, if explained, may actually enhance the public's awareness of the hazard and its ability to process risk information in subsequent warnings.

Fourth, people at risk want information from a mixed set of sources and not from a sole source. Multiple sources help people confirm the warning information and situation, and they help to reinforce belief in the content of the warning message. This does not mean that multiple and different warning messages from different spokespersons are desirable: Warnings work best if different spokespersons all deliver the same message or if a panel of spokespersons delivers the warning a number of times.

Fifth, most people simply do not respond with protective actions to warning messages as soon as they hear their first warning. Most people seek more information about the impending risk and about appropriate responses. This information is usually sought from people who are known and from sources of information other than those who issued the warning in the first place. People call friends, relatives, and neighbors to find out what they plan to do. People also perform a search for additional information in the media. Television is the most-turned-to source in short-term warnings (a few hours to days); written sources such as newspapers are the most turned to sources in longer-term warnings.

Last, most people do not blindly follow instructions in a warning message unless the rationale for the instruction is given in the message, and this explanation must make sense. If instructions in a warning do not make common sense or are not explained, and especially if instructions are absent, people typically behave based on information gathered from other sources or on the way they are predisposed to behave.

But earthquake predictions are not like the warnings issued for hurricanes, tornadoes, and other natural hazards. More often than not they offer probabilities of damaging quakes sometime in the next two or three decades. Longer-term predictions for earthquakes more closely resemble quake education than they resemble warnings for other types of natural hazards. Currently, earthquake predictions are classified as long-term, intermediate-term, and short-term. A long-term prediction may rest on earthquake-potential studies; a short-term prediction would most likely result from much more detailed and specific studies. All three kinds of predictions provide information about earthquake risk and suggest appropriate responses to members of the public, ranging from the purchase of earthquake insurance in the case of a long-term prediction to evacuation after a short-term prediction. It is less likely that a scientifically credible short-term prediction would be made for an area not already classified as having long-term earthquake potential. A long-term classification is almost certainly needed to direct the intensified scientific studies requisite for a short-term prediction.

Under the Disaster Relief Act of 1974, the U.S. Geological Survey has the responsibility to notify appropriate federal, state, and local authorities of earthquake hazards and to provide information as necessary to ensure that timely and effective warnings of potential disasters are provided. The director of the USGS is charged by the Earthquake Hazards Reduction Act of 1977 (as amended in 1980) with authority to issue an earthquake advisory or prediction as deemed necessary. Such an advisory would be issued after the scientific evidence for a prediction is assembled and presented to the National Earthquake Prediction Evaluation Council. Should NEPEC judge that there is scientific merit to a prediction, it would so inform the director of the USGS, who would then issue a prediction to federal, state, and local authorities. Public warnings would then be issued by state offices of emergency services or by county and city authorities.

California has the most detailed prediction-warning plan in the nation. The California Earthquake Prediction Evaluation Council (CEPEC) convenes to advise the governor or the governor's Office of Emergency Services (OES) on the scientific merit of the prediction. It is also planned that USGS, OES, and the California Division of Mines and Geology coordinate the issuance of a prediction. At present, OES informs local counties and cities of a prediction, and OES may participate with them in the preparation and dissemination of emergency information for public distribution. There are plans and procedures for both longer-term earthquake advisories and short-term predictions.

Predictions do not always come from the scientific community; in fact, they are almost routinely offered by psychics and "scientists" on the fringe of the contemporary scientific community. The next chapter reviews the history of earthquake prediction and the history of social scientific research that seeks to understand public prediction response. Where information on social response to a prediction is available, that is also summarized.

4

The Evolution of
Earthquake Warnings

The quest for the technology to predict earthquakes arises from the hope that, someday, the people of the United States can be warned and then do things to protect themselves and their property before quakes strike. The search for ways to predict earthquakes advances science and technology onto new terrain, but the development and evolution of new technology is fraught with difficulty.

Technological innovations . . . function as social change agents because they offer a paradox. Not only do they provide solutions to old dilemmas, they also create new sets of problems with which institutions must cope. The process of adjusting to such circumstances often leads to new institutional arrangements or modification of existing ones (Anderson and Thiel 1979, p. 2).

And once an innovation is introduced, it can impose societal stress until it is incorporated into the ongoing routine of familiar culture. A lack of clarity often prevails as new technologies are developed, and the introduction of a new technology

will often be followed by a period of uncertainty. This results from a lack of adequate knowledge regarding its costs and benefits, how it might be used, and how to integrate it into the existing institutional framework of society (Anderson and Thiel 1979, p. 2).

The United States currently has two bodies that deal with the uncertainties that surround quake predictions as the nation waits for increased technological precision. First, the National Earthquake Prediction Evaluation Council is an outgrowth of the National Earthquake Hazards Reduction Act as passed in 1977 (see Chapter 2). The NEPEC is composed of not fewer than eight federal and nonfederal earth scientists. NEPEC exists to review predictions and data collected by other scientists in order to recommend to the director of the U.S. Geological Survey when a formal earthquake prediction or advisory is warranted. Second, the state of California has its own earthquake prediction evaluation council, which predates NEPEC by about a decade. The California Earthquake Prediction Evaluation Council, headed by the state geologist, serves the same function as NEPEC, but its recommendations are made to the governor through the State Office of Emergency Services.

NEPEC and CEPEC both sift through predictions and eliminate those without scientific merit. And there is potentially much for these gatekeepers to do because quake prediction technology is far from well-refined and developed.

Current Technology

The complexity of earthquake faults makes the task of generating scientific quake predictions extremely difficult (Allen 1982). Current scientific efforts to predict earthquakes involve both estimates of long-term quake probabilities and the considerably more difficult to make estimates of short-term probabilities. And any prediction in the United States must foretell four dimensions about an anticipated quake: (1) the amount of time before the quake is expected, (2) the place or a reasonably specific location, (3) its expected size or magnitude, and (4) its probability or likelihood (Wallace, Davis, and McNally 1984).

Long-term forecasting of great earthquakes with 30-year or so timewindows is fairly well developed, and many people have confidence in the ability of contemporary science to offer these types of forecasts. Intermediate-term and short-term prediction (for quakes within hours, days, weeks, months, and a few years) capabilities are not as far advanced (Wallace, Davis, and McNally 1984). These types of predictions involve an elaborate interplay of methods and techniques. Most approaches seek to detect precursor anomalies that portend an earthquake in the relatively near future. For example, Karen McNally at the University of California at Santa Cruz has developed a statistical modeling method whereby she collects data on swarms of small events in seismic gaps. A seismic gap is a portion of a fault with an obvious lack of quakes, or "quiescence," in its relatively immediate history. These data are then used to calculate shorter-term probabilities for an earthquake in, for example, the next few days to years. Despite encouraging work like that performed by McNally and many others, it is not yet possible for seismologists to routinely

provide a warning immediately before a major earthquake, when it would do the most good. . . . Predicting an earthquake right before it happens would require some recognizable departure from the simple linear accumulation of strain along a segment. Laboratory experiments and theoretical models strongly suggest that we should see preliminary slip on a fault before an earthquake, but they do little to help us estimate either the size or the time of the slip that occurs in real geological materials at the pressures and temperatures found in the earth's crust (Lindh 1990, p. 47).

But Lindh continues with optimism and suggests that with careful monitoring of fault segments and identifying sensitive spots where foreshocks are likely to occur, scientists are hopeful that they can someday learn to "detect, measure, and interpret the signals of a forthcoming earthquake" (Lindh 1990, p. 47).

Earthquake prediction in the United States has a rich and interesting history. Legitimate scientific predictions exist today, but most examples of predictions are of a very different sort. The history and evolution of earthquake prediction involves a broader mix of people than just earth scientists.

Warning History

The earliest evidence of "legitimate" studies to predict earthquakes is among people in ancient Greece and China. The people of these cultures looked for premonitory animal behavior as a way to predict earthquakes. "Historical accounts are rich with reports of strange events before earthquakes: dogs howling, strange lights in the night sky, weird sounds, withdrawal of the sea from a harbor, and so on" (Hamilton 1976, p. 7). In fact, the Chinese organized their citizens to look for premonitory animal behavior as late as the mid-1970s as part of their national earthquake prediction effort.

But modern-day scientific efforts to predict earthquakes began in the early part of this century when the 1906 San Francisco earthquake led scientists to a better understanding of earthquake dynamics.

In the wake of the 1906 San Francisco temblor, Henry Reid proposed that earthquakes are generated by the sudden slip and elastic rebound of crustal blocks bordering a fault. . . . Reid's model, elaborated upon and coupled with the theory of plate tectonics, is the basis for estimating when and where large earthquakes can be expected (Bay Area Regional Earthquake Preparedness Project 1989, p. 6).

The theory of plate tectonics, developed in the 1960s and 1970s (see Chapter 1), helped to explain the process of strain and slip, but the Gilbert-Reid model continues to form the basis of long-term earthquake prediction. This model was built on Grove Karl Gilbert's 1880s view of earthquakes.

Geologists have understood for about 100 years the basic mechanism that produces large earthquakes. Over time, motion on either side of a fault deforms the rock that straddles it. The strain energy accumulates until the rock can no longer contain it, causing slip on the fault. Then, much as tension is released when a coil spring is compressed until its mechanism breaks, energy radiates from the rock adjoining the portion of the fault that slips—which can lead to damage as much as hundreds of miles away. Afterward, the cycle of strain accumulation starts over again (Lindh 1990, p. 45).

The first real step into the contemporary world of earthquake prediction occurred in 1971 at an international scientific meeting in Moscow. Soviet scientists announced that they had learned to recognize some signs that they believed were associated with impending earthquakes. Soviet scientists had been working on prediction techniques for several decades, with particular emphasis on a seismically active region of the Republic of Tadzhikistan. They indicated that the most important sign of an impending earthquake was a change in the velocity of vibrations that pass through the crust of the earth as a result of disturbances such as other earthquakes, underground nuclear tests, or mining blasts.

Earth scientists had long known that vibrations spread outward in two types of seismic waves. The P wave travels at about 3.5 miles a second; it is a longitudinal wave that causes rock particles to expand and contract. The S wave travels at about 2 miles a second near the surface; it causes the earth to move in right angles to the direction of the wave. P waves travel faster than S waves, so they reach seismographs first. The Russian scientists found that the differences in the arrival times of P and S waves begin to decrease markedly for days, weeks, and in some cases, months before an earthquake. Then the wave velocities return to normal shortly before a quake strikes. They also reported that the longer the period of abnormal wave velocity before an earthquake, the larger the ensuing quake.

The Chinese next gave prediction world attention and, perhaps, its most exciting day. In China, "virtually every technique that has ever been suggested as a basis for prediction is being studied to some degree" (Hamilton 1976, p. 8). The Chinese scientists have been successful enough to predict several destructive quakes: the Haicheng earthquake, Liaoning Province, of February 4, 1975; a pair of Richter magnitude 6.9 earthquakes 97 minutes apart near the China-Burma border on May 29, 1976; and a three-event cluster of magnitudes 7.2, 6.7, and 7.2 in the Sungpan-Pingwu, Szechuan Province, on August 14, 22, and 23, 1976. The most important of these predictions was for the Haicheng earthquake. Its prediction had begun some five years earlier.

The State Seismological Bureau (SSB) of China targeted Liaoning Province as a site with potential for a large earthquake, and the area became the focus of more intense investigations by Chinese seismologists. Their examination paid off when the SSB issued a more specific prediction in June 1974. Scientists felt that a quake of about 6.0 magnitude would strike in 1974 or 1975. This statement led to increased scientific investigations, and several thousand amateur observation posts were established to observe well water-levels, animal behavior, radon concentrations in water, and magnetic and electrical phenomena. Then local governments were told to expect a magnitude 5.0 shock on December 20, 1974; two days later there was a 4.8 magnitude quake. Scientists informed officials that a larger quake was still imminent. This prompted the Provincial Revolutionary Committee to step up its efforts to warn and educate the public.

A revised prediction was issued on January 13, 1975, by the SSB, which stated that a magnitude 5.5 to 6.0 quake would strike during the first half of that year in Liaoning Province. Efforts to measure precursory phenomena were again accelerated, and the public prepared to take adaptive action. Increasing seismic activity, a magnitude 4.7 foreshock on the morning of February 4, and reported anomalous well-water and animal behavior observations led the Provincial Revolutionary Committee to issue an alert for a strong earthquake to hit within a two-day time window. Approximately five and one-half hours later a 7.3 magnitude quake struck the area—after the population had evacuated. This prediction and successful public response to it attracted worldwide attention. However, in 1976, an unpredicted 7.8 magnitude quake hit in Tangshan and killed 240,000 people, injured 160,000, and caused billions of yuan in damage.

The Haicheng prediction was not based on theory. Consequently, it did not push the science of prediction in any positive direction. But the usefulness of the prediction from a societal viewpoint has been acclaimed worldwide. For example, Yong (1988) has claimed that the prediction demonstrated just how useful the technology can be as a means to reduce earthquake losses when it is accompanied by public education campaigns. Yong also pointed out that the use of "propaganda" techniques such as the dissemination of popularized earthquake science information; newspaper columns devoted to earthquake prediction and other related matters; drawings on matchbox covers, calendars, and fans; text in middle and primary school books; and summer camps on earthquake science increase public preparedness.

The Chinese were not the only ones who made successful earthquake predictions in the 1970s. For example, successful predictions were also made in the United States. Small quakes were predicted for the Adirondack Mountains region of New York State (Stolz, Sykes, and Aggarwal 1973) and in South Carolina (Stevenson, Talwani, and Amick 1976). The 1974 Thanksgiving Day magnitude 5.2 earthquake near Hollister, California, was also predicted. The U.S. Geological Survey also detected tilt anomalies prior to at least two moderate earthquakes at about this time, but these anomalies gave no information about the expected date of these quakes. A quake in January 1974 was also predicted in southern California as to time and place, but the actual magnitude was less than was predicted.

About this time in the mid-1970s social scientists were drawn into the field of earthquake prediction. This began with an effort to estimate the societal impacts of predictions by the Panel on Public Policy Implications of Earthquake Prediction in the National Research Council of the National Academy of Sciences. The panel was established in 1974, and it used a think-tank approach to ponder the societal issues that would be involved with the prediction of an earthquake. The general conclusion reached by the panel was that there was a significant need to study society's reaction to actual predictions as they were made (Turner, Nigg, and Paz 1986). A study of behavioral intentions in response to hypothetical quake prediction scenarios was performed in 1974 to 1976 (Haas and Mileti 1976; Mileti, Hutton, and Sorensen 1981). The researchers gathered data on what organizational decisionmakers and members of the public thought they might do in response to a scientifically credible prediction. It was concluded that business and community leaders would give credibility to an earthquake prediction and would act on it if (1) the prediction was offered by reputable sources, (2) scientists agreed on the prediction, (3) the prediction expressed certainty regarding the probability of the quake, (4) the prediction was specific about the area of likely impact, and (5) the announcement contained an estimate of the expected quake's magnitude and provided a timewindow. Other major conclusions from this research included that credible scientific predictions of great earthquakes (with time, place, and magnitude specified) in a few months to a few years would create local economic losses of major proportions and that public response would largely be the consequence of what organizations did in response to the prediction. These findings were somewhat mirrored in a major technology assessment of prediction performed by engineers at Stanford Research Institute (Weisbecker *et al.* 1977).

This same group of social scientists also investigated public response to two actual predictions at that time: a scientific prediction for Kawasaki, Japan, and a prediction for Wilmington, North Carolina, by a psychic and her associate—an assistant professor of geology at the University of North Carolina at Chapel Hill. These predictions and the societal research that followed were not landmark work for either the physical or social sciences, but for the first time physical and social scientists had forged an at-arms-length partnership to tread through the science and politics of societal reaction to actual earthquake predictions.

The "scientific" prediction taught some early lessons. The ground under the industrial city of Kawasaki, Japan, began to show signs of crustal deformation and upheaval in 1970. Members of the Coordinating

Committee on Earthquake Prediction (CCEP)—a group of 30 Japanese earth scientists first convened in 1969—decided that the area should be monitored more intensely to determine if the observed upheaval was a precursor to an earthquake. Observations revealed that the upheaval was continuing. Then, in late 1974, the committee recommended that the Kawasaki area be officially designated as a place of intensified study for preearthquake phenomena.

A few members of CCEP viewed the situation as much more serious than did the committee as a whole, and they wanted the available data made public. The information was eventually leaked to a newspaper, and on December 26, 1974, the CCEP was forced to hold a news conference on the topic. It announced that a slowly developing large-scale crustal deformation had been documented in the Kawasaki area. It also stated that although such upheavals are only sometimes associated with earthquakes, it was known that a similar deformation occurred before the 1964 Niigata quake. The CCEP did not announce that an earthquake was likely. But one member of the committee answered with the following when provoked by a news reporter's question: "If an earthquake were associated with the upheaval, it would be 6.2 to 6.4 in magnitude, it would have a shallow epicenter, and it would occur a year later in late 1975 or early 1976." These parameters of the "prediction" made the headlines in the next edition of almost every newspaper in Japan.

Eventually, government and the public reacted in spite of the scientific controversy that surrounded the prediction. The government of Tokyo set up a team to consult with relevant agencies in Kawasaki and Yokohama to establish guidelines for all agencies to follow. In mid-February, Tokyo released damage estimates and related proposals for action. The national Disaster Countermeasures Agency had its budget increased over 25% in order to fund coordination of activities of all the other responding entities. And the governments of Kawasaki and Tokyo began to quarrel over where the likely epicenter would be—both wanted to have it located in their own jurisdictions to increase the power behind their arguments to obtain special readiness funds from the national government. Both governments eventually received national subsidies.

The main fear was that the quake would cause a fire. The national government subsidized research and planning for a segregation belt that was to be constructed to act as a firebreak to protect houses from a possible fire storm in the industrial part of the city.

The social scientists who investigated societal response to the prediction reached several conclusions. For example, earthquake predictions may be acted upon as opportunities by organizations with vested interests; the public did not perceive itself to be at much risk despite all the hoopla in the local press; and prediction response plans would be useful for local government to have before predictions emerged, since plans would reduce the influence of the prevailing political climate on what got done and what was ignored. The CCEP announced in May 1975 that the cultural upheaval was due to industry pumping water out from under the city and then stopping, which caused the land to subside. As more time went by, the area of subsidence experienced an "echo-upheaval," and that was what the CCEP had observed and misinterpreted as a possible signal for a future earthquake. The prediction was called off (Hirose 1985).

Then, in early January 1976, a psychic predicted that a major quake of 8.0 magnitude would strike the Wilmington and Southport areas of North Carolina sometime between January 13 and 20, 1976. Once again, a prediction made front-page news. The psychic's prediction was confirmed by an assistant professor of geology at the University of North Carolina at Chapel Hill. He commented that the psychic's prediction was in agreement with his own scientific findings and that she had successfully predicted the dates of three other earthquakes in the recent past. In fact, the professor published his own prediction in the newspaper on the heels of the psychic's. His companion prediction was for an 8.0 magnitude quake in the same area, but he gave an estimated 10-year time window for the quake.

The professor gave the psychic's prediction scientific credibility. Subsequent societal research showed that about 30% of the population took the time to try to get more information about the prediction; that 40% of the businesses in the area reported a decline in the number of customers, total sales, or both; and that about 6,000 earthquake insurance policies were sold in the area by 85 agents in several days. In fact, three national companies refused to sell any more policies in the area after this overnight increase in sales and financial exposure. About one-third of the public did not take the prediction seriously, but 40% took some sort of action to protect their homes and 17% stockpiled emergency supplies. It was concluded that planning is needed to handle public information after predictions, since people seemed to react to the prediction on the basis of the perceptions they formed from the information they received. The quake did not happen, and the nontenured assistant professor of geology was eventually asked to leave the university.

The first large-scale empirical research on an actual earthquake forecast in the United States began in early February 1976 when the U.S. Geological Survey reported that a land uplift—not unlike the uplift discovered in Kawasaki—about 25 centimeters in height was detected along a portion of the San Andreas fault just north of Los Angeles. The uplift was centered near the town of Palmdale in the Mojave Desert. The USGS stated that the uplift was not fully understood and that it might or might not be a precursor to an earthquake. The USGS expressed concern because the uplift was along a section of the San Andreas fault that had been inactive since the great 1857 Fort Tejon earthquake. This uplift phenomenon came to be known as the Palmdale Bulge; it covered about 4,500 square miles in 1976 and grew to 32,000 square miles by 1980 (Mileti, Hutton, and Sorensen 1981).

The mass media in southern California drew the public's attention to the discovery of the uplift along with news of a devastating earthquake in Guatemala. USGS seismologists and other scientists did not fully understand the meaning of the uplift, but they did express considerable concern that it could be a precursor to an earthquake. They thought the uplift serious enough to warrant giving a full briefing to the governor of California. "While acknowledging the uncertain meaning of the uplift, the California Seismic Safety Commission officially declared on April 8 that "the uplift should be considered a threat to public safety and welfare in the Los Angeles metropolitan area" (Turner, Nigg, and Paz 1986, p. 7).

News of the Palmdale Bulge led a team of four social scientists (Turner *et al.* 1978) to assess societal reaction. The researchers classified the announcement as an "approximate prediction," since neither the place, time, nor magnitude was precisely stated. Their investigation was intended "as a first step toward understanding how communities respond to the announcement of near predictions, and by inference, how they may respond to earthquake predictions in the future" (Turner, Nigg, and Paz 1986, p. 6).

The research demonstrated that few people were seriously concerned about the quake and little household preparedness occurred even though nearly everyone believed that the quake was coming soon. The study also discovered that people who heard about the announcement from scientific sources took it more seriously than did those who heard about it from nonscientific sources. The announcement induced the public to engage in a search for additional information. For example, as the event unfolded and as each new development led to more media coverage, people would request speakers to address schools, service clubs, or church groups, and they typically called local and familiar emergency organizations such as fire and police departments (Turner *et al.* 1978). Overall, the information did not precipitate negative economic impacts, as those who had done prior work on societal reaction to prediction had suspected, but neither were many positive public reactions observed.

In April 1976, a seismologist from a California university predicted that a 5.5 to 6.5 Richter magnitude earthquake would strike the San Fernando, California, area north of Los Angeles sometime in the next 12 months, and the prediction was widely covered by local newspapers. Even though the scientist was cautious to not label his forecast a prediction (but rather a hypothesis test) "to the media and the public, this distinction was not evident" (Mileti, Hutton, and Sorensen 1981, p. 33). The Los Angeles City Council moved within a week of the announcement to evaluate the legal implications of possible declining property values resulting from the prediction, and several insurance companies "stopped or delayed selling new earthquake policies. One company canceled earthquake coverage on all its homeowners' policies that were in force" (Mileti, Hutton, and Sorensen 1981, p. 33).

> Public appraisals of and responses to the prediction were clarified by institutional mechanisms designed to determine quickly the credibility of the prediction and the seriousness of the threat. The scientific evidence for the prediction was submitted to the California Earthquake Prediction Evaluation Council for review. . . . The council concluded that there was not sufficient evidence to warrant an official prediction announcement. In late 1976, the author of the prediction indicated that new data had led him to conclude that the hypothesis ("prediction") had not been supported by the data. In effect, what had been described in the media as a prediction was then withdrawn (Mileti, Hutton, and Sorensen 1981, p. 33).

The southern California news media deluged the public with information about the hypothesis test, and about earthquakes in general. That year the city of Los Angeles drew up and adopted the first prediction response plan in the country.

Social scientists at the University of California at Los Angeles surveyed residents of the Los Angeles area to monitor trends in attitudes, perceptions, and responses to all the "prediction" information that was circulated (Turner 1983; Turner, Nigg, and Paz 1986). They found that as time passed, people tended to notice or remember less and less information about earthquake hazards. This finding raised interesting questions about the saturation point beyond which a public could not take in additional information, and about the relationship between information redundancy and a public's attention span. But these ideas have never been validated in subsequent studies.

Most important, the researchers found that channels of information on which people relied changed over time. At first, people tended to rely more on television than on newspapers, but as time passed they relied more on newspapers than on television. Personal and household preparedness actions were also found to be a function of time. Preparedness actions increased when information was new but decreased as time passed (Turner 1983).

It was time to take stock of what had been learned about the societal aspects of prediction. The National Research Council of the National Academy of Sciences issued another report in 1978 by the Committee on Socioeconomic Effects of Earthquake Prediction. It foretold social and economic disruptions from scientifically credible predictions for large earthquakes. The jury on this topic should have been split, since the data gathered up to that point described predictions with only minor impacts, and without any ensuing societal dislocations. The report also presented a detailed research agenda for future societal prediction research.

In 1980, two American scientists, Brady and Spence, predicted an earthquake in Lima, Peru, for the summer of 1981. The former scientist's affiliation with the U.S. Bureau of Mines and the latter's with the U.S. Geological Survey gave the prediction credibility. Several assessments of the socioeconomic consequences of the prediction were performed. Researchers Olson, Podesta, and Nigg (1989) concluded that the prediction precipitated a fierce political controversy. And Echevarria, Norton, and Norton (1986, p. 175) concluded that, "over half of the population of Lima took some precautionary measures, that the total economic damage for the prediction was roughly $50 million, and that the poorer groups in society bore a disproportionate share of the prediction costs."

At last, some detailed empirical support was discerned for the idea that predictions can be quite disruptive to society if they are not well managed. In hindsight, it appears that long-term predictions (as that with the Palmdale Bulge) are readily handled and easily made productive for society; short-term predictions (such as the North Carolina and Haicheng predictions) are quite manageable from a societal viewpoint and somewhat analogous to hurricane warnings; however, intermediate-term predictions (as was the case with the Kawasaki and Peru predictions) can be problematic to communities without prediction response and public information plans.

In a review of social science research reports on disasters outside the United States, Robert Stallings (1982) proposed major variables important to consider in determining whether a given group of people will believe an earthquake prediction. He focused on credibility (the probability that public statements about future earthquake events are believed) and the prediction dissemination process and came to the following conclusions. People are more likely to believe scientific earthquake predictions when they overlap or converge with nonscientific forecasts. Belief in a prediction will vary along ethnic, social class, and age lines. Credibility is shaped by the general sense of trust that people have in government when prediction information is released by governmental authorities. In fatalistic cultures, predictions may be viewed as credible, but preparedness actions do not necessarily follow. And,

the nature of the prediction itself may have some influence on its credibility. Predictions may be stated either in terms of the likelihood of an earthquake in a certain place during a certain period of time, or of the absence of earthquakes above a certain magnitude in a region between two points in time. There is some indication that predictions of the former type (of the presence of some event) are inherently more credible than those of the latter type (of the absence of some event) (Stallings 1982, p. 65).

Stallings's insights were important for the time because he opened the door for others to look across prediction events for discernible patterns on which to build a foundation for public policy. Notwithstanding its usefulness, his work was largely ignored at the time.

The investigation of the societal aspects of prediction continued in the early 1980s. But there were few actual predictions issued to study. The earth sciences community retreated to more confined studies in the 1980s. Nonetheless, Roberts, Milliman, and Ellson (1982) conducted a simulated economic study using a modified regional econometric model to estimate the impact of a credible prediction in the Charleston, South Carolina, region. The major conclusion from this work was that a prediction, whether correct or false, would dampen the economy but that an unanticipated quake might ultimately boost the economy.

By the mid-1980s new actors had arrived on the scene. The new crop of physical scientists were young and energetic and simply spoke their minds. This posture led to the issuance of a raftfull of a new sort of short-term predictions issued after unpredicted earthquakes. This type of prediction is based on the idea that the odds of a larger quake are up after a smaller one has already happened. An early example of this sort of prediction was the 1985 San Diego earthquake prediction.

This prediction was issued after a swarm of earthquakes on the Rose Canyon fault in June 1985. There were three quakes with magnitudes of 4.0, 4.2, and 4.0 on the seventeenth of the month. Seismologists at the USGS field office at Cal Tech conferred with their headquarters in Reston, Virginia, and they "agreed that there was a slight increase in the probability of a potentially damaging earthquake in the San Diego metropolitan area" (Southern California Earthquake Preparedness Project 1985, p. 3). They estimated that the probability of this 5.0-magnitude-or-greater quake was about 5% in the following five days.

San Diego County first learned of the prediction through informal means. Neither the county nor any of the six cities in the area had prediction response plans. In hindsight, the city disaster coordinators agreed that prediction response plans would have reduced a lot of the uncertainty they had about what to do when they were presented with the prediction. Eventually, California developed its own plan in 1990, along with strong recommendations that all cities in the state do the same.

The most recent example of postearthquake predictions of subsequent quakes comes from the 1989 Loma Prieta. The earthquake came as no surprise to scientists; its occurrence as well as its major effects were anticipated.

The Loma Prieta earthquake ruptured a segment of the San Andreas fault in the Santa Cruz Mountains that had been recognized as early as 1983 as having a high probability for rupture in the following few decades. In a study in 1988, this segment was assigned the highest probability for producing a M 6.5 to 7 earthquake of any California fault segment north of the Los Angeles metropolitan area (U.S. Geological Survey Staff 1990, p. 286).

Public aftershock warnings were issued during the emergency and for two months thereafter. The first warning was issued at 7:15 a.m. on October 18. It stated,

An analysis of historical earthquake sequences in the past 50 years in California suggests that there is a 1 to 2 in 10 (10% to 20%) probability of a M6 or larger aftershock in the first 24 hours following the mainshock and diminishing thereafter (U.S. Geological Survey 1989a, p. 1).

A different warning appeared in the *San Francisco Examiner* for the same time period (October 18, 1989). It reported a possibility for a 7.0 magnitude aftershock in the first 24 hours following the mainshock. The USGS did state that there was a possibility for a 7.0 magnitude quake on an adjacent fault in the first 24 hours after the mainshock. It declared,

Although the likelihood is remote, there is also a possibility of a M7 or greater earthquake in the coming days on an adjacent segment of the San Andreas Fault (U.S. Geological Survey 1989a, p. 1).

Another aftershock warning was issued for the 24-to-48-hour period after the mainshock at 5:00 p.m. on October 18. It stated:

As of Wednesday at 5:00 p.m. PDT, there is only a 2 percent chance of a magnitude 6.0 or larger aftershock in the next 24 hours. In the same period, the probability of a magnitude 5.0 or larger aftershock is 13 percent (U.S. Geological Survey 1989b, p. 2).

A third aftershock warning was issued on October 21, three days after the mainshock. This warning was made public at 7:00 a.m.; it reduced the probability of a 5.0 magnitude aftershock to 8 percent.

At this time there is only about a one percent chance of a magnitude 6 or larger aftershock in the 24-hour period beginning at 7:00 a.m. PDT today.

The chance of a magnitude 5 or larger aftershock in the same 24-hour period is eight percent (U.S. Geological Survey 1989c, p. 2).

Finally, one full week after the earthquake, the USGS issued another warning, which was in effect for the balance of the year.

Seismologists advise that additional aftershocks are expected in the next few weeks to months, some possibly strong enough to cause additional damage, especially to structures weakened in last Tuesday's quake (U.S. Geological Survey 1989d, p. 1).

Public reaction to these predictions was studied in detail (Fitzpatrick and Mileti 1990; Mileti and O'Brien 1992). The researchers discovered that many people did many things to prepare for damaging aftershocks, but it was observed that those who had losses in the mainshock did the most to prepare for aftershocks, and that those who had few or no mainshock losses did very little to get ready. They concluded that the public may be prone to a "normalization" bias when it comes to interpreting aftershock predictions: People interpret their risk to predicted aftershocks in line with their experience in the mainshock and not in ways consistent with the actual risks they may face.

In December 1989, a quake prediction was made that may well be the most infamous to date; it bore an uncanny resemblance to the Wilmington, North Carolina, prediction of 1976. The USGS has been investigating the seismic characteristics of the central United States for several years, and USGS seismologists estimate that there is a 13 to 65 percent chance that the New Madrid, Missouri, fault will produce a major earthquake by the year 2000 (Edwards 1991).

However, in December 1989 when Iben Browning, a climatologist and business consultant from New Mexico, aired his controversial prediction for a 6.5 to 7.5 magnitude earthquake on the New Madrid fault on December 3, 1990, give or take 48 hours, only then did this earthquake-prone area receive focused media and public attention. Very significantly, legitimate scientific groups of earth scientists stepped forward to defuse what most thought to be a bogus prediction.

On December 12, 1989, about two months after a powerful earthquake struck San Francisco, the Missouri Governor's Conference on Agriculture met in Osage Beach, Mo., a town in the southwest Missouri Ozarks. One of the speakers at that meeting was Iben Browning, a New Mexico climatologist. Browning claimed to have predicted the San Francisco earthquake, and also "projected" at the Missouri meeting that the New Madrid Fault area, which runs from just south of St. Louis, to about Marked Tree, Ark., which is about 30 miles northwest of Memphis, was a prime area for an earthquake in early December, 1990. . . . In the next 12 months

Browning's name would become a household word for many in parts of Missouri, Kentucky, Illinois, Tennessee and Arkansas. His prediction led to many public meetings, to disaster preparedness drills, to school closings, to self-evacuation by some residents in the area and to national media coverage as the earthquake prediction date neared (Shipman, Fowler, and Shain 1991, p. 1).

The Browning prediction was given credibility by a local earth scientist (the very same person who, as an assistant professor at the University of North Carolina at Chapel Hill, gave credibility to the psychic's prediction in 1976) and then it was given considerable attention by the mass media. The media issued what could be considered a public earthquake warning. The prediction was extensively studied by social scientists.

The prediction was widely believed by the public (Farley *et al.* 1991). And it was the media who played the key role in shaping people's perceptions (Atwood 1991). More than anything else, the 12-month-long widespread news coverage of the prediction "led to a heightened awareness of the problem of earthquakes in general and especially of the possibility of a major quake along the New Madrid Fault Line" (Baldwin 1991, p. 1). In addition, the prediction prompted people to take earthquake readiness actions, for example, to purchase earthquake insurance. It also prompted some organizations, such as schools and banks, to change routine operating procedures on the day the earthquake was supposed to occur (Edwards 1991; Farley *et al.* 1991; Kennedy 1991). Members of the public did not change daily routines as a direct result of the prediction (Sylvester 1991), but the prediction response actions of organizations caused citizens to alter daily schedules (Farley *et al.* 1991).

A number of explanations have been offered for this bogus prediction's becoming salient to the public. First, Browning was strongly supported by the director of the Center for Earthquake Studies at Southeast Missouri State University (Edwards 1991): "It is clear that up to half of the public did not see scientists as clearly rejecting the Browning forecast, despite the statements of both individual scientists and scientist groups to that effect" (Farley *et al.* 1991, p. 32). Second, "the Loma Prieta earthquake occurred a year earlier, and this increased awareness of the quake threat throughout the American collective consciousness" (Baldwin 1991, p. 1). Third, local businesses helped to make the prediction salient when they took advantage of the situation to market quake-related products. Fourth, emergency management agencies also found, "an opportunity to place earthquake safety issues on the public agenda" (Edwards 1991, p. 19) and conducted campaigns to increase community hazard awareness and preparedness. This lent credibility to Browning and increased the visibility and legitimacy of the prediction (Edwards 1991). Finally, less than three months before the predicted major quake, a Richter magnitude

4.6 quake hit in the region, and it was felt over a wide area and received considerable media attention (Baldwin 1991). This seemingly innocuous event undoubtedly contributed to making the Browning prediction even more salient than might have otherwise been the case.

Obviously, the history of earthquake prediction over the past several decades is peppered with successes and failures. But the science of quake prediction is being advanced, societal research is keeping pace, and applications to enhance societal readiness are too numerous to mention. "As the ability of scientists to predict earthquakes improves, such forecasting capability will likely be put to even increased use" (Governor's Board of Inquiry 1990, p. 91). The belief by many scientists that there will be a highly destructive great earthquake in a densely populated area of the country in the near future leaves us wishing well to those who would develop successful prediction capabilities.

The most scientifically approved and credible earthquake prediction in the United States and, perhaps, the world has yet to be described: the great Parkfield, California earthquake prediction experiment is being conducted in the central part of California. The next chapter gives an account of this prediction, and then Chapter 6 details the results of what may be the most comprehensive societal study of public reaction to an earthquake prediction ever performed.

5

The Parkfield Prediction, the Warning
and the People at Risk

Earthquake predictions and warnings are certainly not new phenomena. They have surfaced in one form or another since time immemorial. Recent historical predictions have emanated from legitimate scientists, sometimes from psychics, and other times they have come from a combination of the two. But national policy to deal with predictions is relatively new to the American scene. Currently, under the guidelines established by the National Earthquake Hazards Reduction Program, the responsibility for predictions in our nation lies in the hands of the U.S. Geological Survey, the National Earthquake Prediction Evaluation Council and the California Earthquake Prediction Evaluation Council for predictions that emerge in that state.

The Parkfield earthquake prediction experiment is the first earthquake prediction and warning to ever surface in the United States that has been sanctioned by the NEPEC and CEPEC. Based on historical recurrence evidence, the Parkfield earthquake prediction is for a moderate earthquake of 5.5 to 6.0 Richter magnitude on the Parkfield segment of the San Andreas fault between 1985 and 1993. The quake is given a 90% probability of occurrence. Contained in the prediction is the possibility that the next Parkfield earthquake could be magnitude 7.0. The larger event could offset the fault by 10 feet but the characteristic 5.0 to 6.0 magnitude event would likely offset the fault by only one foot. If the larger earthquake, happened there could be damage up to 40 miles from the point of fault rupture. This would mean considerable damage to poorly constructed buildings from near the California coast to the central San Joaquin Valley.

The Prediction Experiment

The experiment began when William Bakun and Al Lindh (two USGS scientists) submitted data to the National Earthquake Prediction Evaluation Council on November 16, 1984. The NEPEC endorsed the prediction and agreed that the director of the USGS should be advised to issue a statement about the prediction. The NEPEC agreed that this statement should contain reference to a significant potential for the larger earthquake and its associated rupture to occur. The CEPEC met on February 13, 1985, and agreed with the high probability for a magnitude 6.0 earthquake. The director of the USGS issued a public statement announcing the prediction on April 5, 1985. It was titled "Studies Forecasting Moderate Earthquake near Parkfield, California Receive Official Endorsement" and it is presented in Appendix A. The statement told that the forecasted earthquake's magnitude was likely to be 5.5 to 6.0, that the quake would happen sometime between 1985 and 1993, and that it had a 90% probability of occurrence; the announcement also noted the potential for the quake to be larger and for the fault rupture to extend into the adjacent San Andreas fault.

The release of this prediction was a national media event. The media descended on the town of Parkfield to interview all of its 36 residents. Stories of the prediction were carried around the world, and the population of Parkfield and people in other likely to be affected cities were immersed in a sea of public information about the prediction and what to do to get ready for the quake. This intense flow of information began the day that the director of the USGS made his announcement, it continued for years to come and it still continues. To date no new or revised Parkfield prediction has been issued, nor has the earthquake occurred.

The Parkfield prediction is more than a simple forecast of an earthquake. This segment of the San Andreas fault is one of the most researched and instrumented fault areas in the world. It is classified as an experiment because it is also an attempt by geological and seismological scientists to detect short-term anomalies that might foretell an earthquake a few days beforehand. Therein lies the hope that such anomalies would indicate the quake's occurrence within a 72-hour period and a short-term public warning could be issued.

A wide array of instruments have been placed in the Parkfield region, all of which represent the concerted effort of many researchers to advance the science of earthquake prediction. Scientists are gathering data on the occurrence of smaller earthquakes in the region to search for patterns that might foretell the predicted Parkfield event. The fault is being examined for creep to see if land movement in the area expected to be the epicenter for the quake indicates that it is soon due. Deformation of the ground is being investigated with a variety of types of strain meters to detect the impending quake. Fluctuations of groundwater levels in a network of wells near Parkfield are being monitored. The ground in the area is being examined with meters to detect tilts in the earth that might foretell instability in the materials near the surface. Local magnetic fields are being monitored for changes due to increased stress associated with an impending earthquake. Changes in electrical currents in the earth and in receptivity associated with concentrations in stress are being examined. Scientists are monitoring radio frequency transmissions in the area to test whether such signals precede the anticipated earthquake. Two-color lasers are used to determine rises and deflations in the height of the earth's surface on the fault. Many other such state-of-the-art technologies are being used to accumulate information that might lead scientists to conclude that the impending Parkfield event is near at-hand (Lindh 1990).

The scientific interest in the next Parkfield earthquake goes well beyond the prediction. "In addition to the elements of the prediction experiment, geophysical instrumentation is being deployed near Parkfield that will take advantage of the predicted features of the coming earthquake to address specific outstanding issues of earthquake mechanics (Bakun and Lindh 1985, p. 623)." Furthermore, efforts similar to those at Parkfield, while not as heavily instrumented as Parkfield, are ongoing in various parts of the nation and around the world.

The Warning

The Parkfield area is a good place to conduct prediction experiments because an earthquake occurs there on the average of almost every 22 years. The 22 year phenomenon is known as the "characteristic Parkfield earthquake." Records and reports by local residents indicate that earthquakes happened there in 1857, in 1881, in 1901, and then again in 1922, 1934, and 1966. Neither scientists nor residents doubt that the central portion of California's Cholame Valley, which contains Parkfield, is earthquake country.

The actual Parkfield prediction would have likely gone unnoticed by the residents of Parkfield and its environs because the people who live there know that quakes happen often. But the national media focused attention on the prediction because of the NEPEC and CEPEC endorsements. The prediction was not even considered very newsworthy by local area newspapers. For example, the *Daily Press*, the local newspaper for northern San Luis Obispo County, did not even run a story on it. This paper covered some earthquake stories that related to Earthquake Preparedness Week in California about two weeks after the forecast came out, for example, it covered an earthquake drill in Los Angeles and stories about the 1906 San Francisco earthquake. Not until May 1985 did the *Daily Press* cover earthquake research activities in Parkfield and explain that the area's history of earthquake activity attracted scientists to do research there. Interestingly, the focus of the news coverage was on the scientists and the fact that research activity going on in the local area, and not about concern over an impending earthquake.

Nevertheless, the prediction did not go unnoticed by local residents. Like the rest of the world, locals learned about the prediction from the coverage that appeared on the national media. This coverage seemed to affect local residents in two ways. First, locals did in fact talk more about earthquakes in Parkfield than they would have had the prediction not been issued, but their attention to the prediction was not the consequence of there being a Parkfield prediction announcement. Instead, it was the consequence of there being so many members of the news media in the area asking questions about the prediction and what residents were thinking and doing. For a short time there were more members of the media in the town of Parkfield to interview residents than there were residents. Second, children in the local one-room schoolhouse had earthquake-related issues made part of their daily lessons, but this too was more in response to the presence of members of the national media than the to prediction itself. School lessons on earthquakes were essentially an attempt by the local teacher to educate children so that they might not become scared from all the questions being asked of them by national reporters (Mileti and Hutton 1986).

The prediction announcement was not newsworthy in Parkfield because the story was not interesting; residents of the area had also noticed that earthquakes tend to occur there every 22 years or so, and stories about past earthquakes are very much a part of local culture and folklore. Telling them something they already knew would not be news. Additionally, most of the people who live in Parkfield had become friendly with the researchers working in the area. They had learned about the scientific aspects of the prediction in the course of conversations with researchers, and these conversations occurred long before the USGS announcement had ever been issued.

This is not to say that steps were not taken to inform residents in Parkfield and other places at risk about the quake they faced, and to advise them on what to do about it. The California Office of Emergency Services took two major actions to communicate the risk and provide advise on what to do. First, the OES initiated a monthly Parkfield earthquake prediction exercise with disaster response officials in the area at risk. Second, the state prepared and mailed a brochure to people's homes that described the prediction and contained recommendations on actions that people could take to get ready. The brochure was mailed to the more than 122,000 central California households within the extended area at risk—the area that would be affected by the earthquake if it turned out to be 7.0 magnitude.

In February 1988 the state initiated its prediction exercises with local offices of emergency services. These exercises were first a means of keeping the prediction salient in the prolonged absence of an earthquake and second they were a way of maintaining an awareness level in local staff in spite of personnel turnover. Earthquake prediction drills involved communication sequences that will be initiated whenever a 72-hour earthquake warning is issued. The USGS notifies the governor's OES, which in turn notifies county offices of emergency services. These county offices have developed their own approaches to notifying other local area agencies.

The brochure that was mailed directly to the 122,000 at-risk households covered information about the earthquake hazard, the prediction, a possible short-term warning of the impending earthquake, and what to do about each. Titled "The Parkfield Earthquake Prediction", the brochure looked like a large folded map. It was color printed on both sides and it presented graphic and textual information concerning the earthquake risk. Concentric circles depicted the areas of potential impact, and pictures and diagrams showed the warning sequence for the short-term warning.

The brochure explained that Parkfield was the epicenter for moderately damaging earthquakes in 1922, 1934, and 1966 and that damage from these quakes primarily consisted of broken windows, chimneys, walls, and glassware. It contained a further message that the next Parkfield quake could possibly be larger than the characteristic magnitude 6.0 quake, although scientists thought that this was much less likely than one the same size.

The brochure explained that the USGS would review data from instruments located near Parkfield and would monitor "alert levels" of the various probabilities that an earthquake was imminent. When "alert level A" is reached, the procedure is for the USGS to issue to the state a short-term earthquake prediction: that the USGS believes there is a 37% chance of a magnitude 6.0 earthquake near Parkfield any time within the next 72-hour period.

The brochure contained information about what people should do during the 72-hour warning period, during the earthquake, and immediately afterward. The recommended actions included storing food and water, assembling an emergency kit, inspecting homes and workplaces for hazards such as unsecured water heaters and bookcases, preparing a home emergency plan, learning emergency plans at schools and workplaces, maintaining a fire extinguisher and reserve supply of medications, participating in neighborhood earthquake readiness programs, and obtaining additional readiness materials from other organizations. Listed in the brochure were names and telephone numbers of key organizations the public could contact for more information, such as county emergency services offices and the state OES Sacramento headquarters. The brochure indicated that during the 72-hour warning period, people should stay in touch with media information, use the brochure itself as a guide, check emergency supplies, discuss the impending earthquake with others to review personal protective measures, note any special needs of family members and neighbors, and review their family emergency plans. Also presented was an explanation about the Richter scale of earthquake magnitudes along with a detailed description of the Modified Mercalli scale, which reflects ground-shaking intensity from earthquakes.

The Places at Risk

Many places in central California could be affected by the next Parkfield earthquake, especially if it is the larger 7.0 magnitude. The communities of Parkfield, Avenal, Coalinga, San Miguel, and Paso Robles could be shaken severely (Modified Mercalli shaking intensity VIII) in the next Parkfield earthquake. Shaking intensity VIII damage is described as follows: "slight in specially designed structures; considerable in ordinary substantial buildings with partial collapse; great in poorly built structures. Panel walls thrown out of frame structures. Fall of chimneys, factory stacks, columns, monuments, walls. Heavy furniture overturned. Sand and mud ejected in small amounts. Changes in the condition of well water." Atascadero and Taft are potentially prone to experiencing up to shaking intensity VII. Shaking intensity VII is described as follows: "Damage negligible in buildings of good design and construction; slight to moderate in well-built ordinary structures; considerable in poorly built or badly designed structures; some chimneys broken. Noticed by persons driving motor cars." The larger communities of Bakersfield, Hanford, Fresno, Hollister, Monterey, and even parts of Santa Barbara County are also subject to effects from the next Parkfield earthquake.

Parkfield

The Parkfield community has an "earthquake culture". Parkfield residents have incorporated the risk of earthquakes into their local belief systems and norms. Resulting perceptions and behaviors include not only recognition and acceptance of earthquake risk but also ideas about what to do to "successfully" live with the risk and how to survive the earthquakes.

Earthquakes are both experienced and anticipated by residents of Parkfield. They are expected and defined as much as a part of living in the area as is true for any other local characteristic. The earthquake hazard and ideas about what to do are such a strong component of local culture that the belief system surrounding the hazard is passed on from generation to generation in much the same way as other more basic cultural traits transcend and are shared across generations.

That people in Parkfield and its immediate surroundings have incorporated the earthquake hazard into their local culture is not a surprise. Earthquakes help mark time for people in Parkfield, and many residents recollect the 1966 event either because they were there or because others have told them about it. It is common folk knowledge, based on the historical record of the characteristic Parkfield earthquake, that quakes occur every now and then and that more should be anticipated in the future. In this way the residents of Parkfield and its surrounding areas have also incorporated earthquake prediction into their local culture—most people presume that earthquakes will occur in their lifetimes. The historical track record of earthquake occurrences provide a standing folk prediction that the locals understand and accept.

The earthquake culture in Parkfield goes beyond the mere acceptance and anticipation of earthquakes: It also clearly defines and limits the risk. Local residents estimate the loss in future Parkfield earthquakes on the basis of prior events experienced and recollected. Relatively recent events—recent in the sense that their intensity, magnitude, and impact are a part of the collective knowledge shared by residents—have not posed a serious threat to life and property; consequently, people believe that future earthquake events won't either. People have kept cupboard doors in kitchens tied shut in anticipation of a future earthquake with its anticipated minimal damage. People take pride that their homes are able to withstand Parkfield quakes; they even reassure one another that it is safer to live closer to the San Andreas fault, as they do, because damage, in their minds, would likely be higher further away—the San Andreas Fault runs under the bridge at the entrance to the town.

Given Parkfield earthquake culture, it is quite understandable why the April 5, 1985, prediction went virtually unnoticed by local residents. A conversation with a Parkfield resident soon after the April 5 announcement summed up the local viewpoint: "When scientists started doing research on earthquakes around here, that meant scientists finally realized what we always knew: earthquakes happen here. When that panel of government people issued their prediction, that just meant that government finally noticed too" (Mileti and Hutton 1986). However, the earthquake culture that is so much a part of daily life for the few people who live in Parkfield does not extend to the other communities at risk for the predicted Parkfield quake. Communities like Coalinga, Paso Robles, and Taft have their own unique characteristics and reasons to be aware or unaware of the earthquake hazard.

Coalinga

Coalinga originated as a loading point for the Southern Pacific Railroad and was known as Coaling Station A in the late 1800s. In 1906 it officially incorporated as the city of Coalinga. The Coalinga Chamber of Commerce in 1910 declared this town and its surrounding areas as the greatest oil field in the United States. The Kettleman Hills and Coalinga Nose oil fields are still in operation. Coalinga's oil fields have provided it with a permanent set of homes, businesses, and other establishments. Located about 18 miles east of Parkfield, Coalinga is easily accessible by the Golden State Freeway. Los Angeles is about 200 miles to the south and San Francisco, about 160 miles to the north. Fresno is the closest city of any appreciable size.

Coalinga residents have good reason to be aware of earthquakes: In 1983 a magnitude 6.7 earthquake struck Coalinga at 4:42 p.m. on May 2. This earthquake was centered ten kilometers northeast of town and caused considerable damage to the buildings of Coalinga. No deaths resulted, but almost 200 people were injured with 20 of those seriously. There was more than 31 million dollars in property damage, and about one-third of the town's 2,700 homes, many of them unattached to their foundations, were lost in the 28 second-long quake. Coalinga's downtown, an area of one- and two-story unreinforced masonry buildings constructed between 1909 and 1940, virtually collapsed. The quake created a dust cloud which enveloped the entire community and limited visibility to 500 feet. Several people were trapped or struck by fallen masonry. A fire erupted in a collapsed building in the downtown area. Local phone service and electrical power failed and police department and hospital radios went off the air.

The initial quake was followed by 10 major aftershocks within a 12-hour period. Ground motion was almost continuous, and a seismograph located at West Hill Community College consumed a week's supply of ink in five hours. Even though aftershocks hindered emergency response, the injured were removed to hospitals and the fires brought under control in a very timely manner.

The major social impacts of the Coalinga earthquake on the community remain. Downtown Coalinga is now composed of completely new buildings, with no historic buildings in evidence. The earthquake became an historical benchmark for the residents of Coalinga. People talk about events as taking place before and after the earthquake. Since 1983, Coalinga community leaders have tried to revive Coalinga physically and psychologically. These attempts have been aimed at convincing the outside world that Coalinga has been restored and is a prospering city. Indeed, the population of Coalinga grew from approximately 7,000 at the time of the 1983 earthquake to about 8,000 in late 1988, largely as a result of increased oil and farming activities and the new prison located in nearby Avenal.

The 1983 Coalinga earthquake also stimulated a great deal of public information campaigns to help the residents of the area be better prepared for future earthquakes. For example, the schools in Coalinga have earthquake plans that staff and teachers are required to read once a year. The schools also hold "duck and cover" drills once a month. Schools have evacuation drills with a buddy system for staff and students, and children have walking routes that they always use to go home so that they can be located by their parents should another quake ever strike at that time of day. Each school has rendezvous areas with disaster kits including buckets, crowbars, and other basic tools. The schools also distribute coloring books about earthquakes and how to get ready for them.

Neighborhood Watch organizations got information to the citizens, particularly about earthquake recovery and fire suppression. The women's club put out information on the earthquake hazard and on preparedness a few years after the 1983 quake. The county health department held puppet shows for children after the earthquake to promote discussion and venting of feelings about it. The telephone company inserted in its telephone book a page indicating actions to take in the event of an earthquake. Pacific Gas and Electric Company, along with General Telephone put on public earthquake preparedness presentations for the residents of Coalinga.

Despite Coalinga's relatively recent experience with a damaging earthquake, or possibly because of it, the Parkfield earthquake prediction was not welcomed by Coalinga residents; they seem to want to forget about earthquakes. However, a variety of information sources informed the Coalinga residents about the Parkfield earthquake prediction. Fresno County (the county in which Coalinga is located) officials started the process of public education about the prediction some six months after the Parkfield prediction was first issued. They held press conferences on the prediction and told medical personnel how to get more information. These officials have also told other groups about the Parkfield prediction: the U.S. Forest Service, the California Division of Forestry, the U.S. Department of Agriculture, the California Highway Patrol, California State University in Fresno, and varied police and fire departments.

Paso Robles

Paso Robles, another community at risk for the Parkfield earthquake, is located about halfway between San Francisco and Los Angeles on Highway 101, approximately 25 miles from Parkfield as the crow flies.

The area is marked by rolling hills and valleys with an average elevation between 600 and 1,900 feet. The Santa Lucia Mountain Range protects the valley on the west and the south, and the Cholame Hills are to the east. Nearby communities include San Luis Obispo (the county seat of San Luis Obispo County, in which Paso Robles lies); Atascadero which has a zoo for endangered species; and Morro Bay with its harbor and beaches.

Tourism is an important element of the Paso Robles area economy; there are opportunities for fishing and water skiing on nearby lakes and deep-sea fishing on the coast and visiting California missions. Vineyards were introduced into the area in 1797 by Franciscan missionaries at San Miguel Archangel. From small beginnings, the area grew to have more than 20 wineries with more than 6,000 planted acres.

Between 1980 and 1987 the Paso Robles growth rate was seven to eight percent per year; the 1989 population was approximately 17,000. Many of its newcomers are from Los Angeles and San Francisco and are seeking a quieter life-style. According to city officials, these newcomers were responsible for precipitating planning for earthquake preparedness in Paso Robles because they were familiar with earthquake plans in the larger communities from which they had moved, and they were concerned about earthquake preparedness in their new homes.

San Luis Obispo county officials responsible for emergency services for Paso Robles have also developed emergency response plans in connection with the nearby Diablo Canyon Nuclear Power Plant. The county developed a public information function geared toward large-scale disasters as a result of the power plant's proximity.

There has also been a considerable number of earthquake and earthquake preparedness stories in most of the newspapers serving the people of Paso Robles. Paso Robles is also served by three television stations, three cable stations, and 16 radio stations. A typical family in Paso Robles has probably been exposed to a multiplicity of information on earthquakes in the Parkfield prediction, mostly on television. The most active television station covering earthquake risk in the Paso Robles area was an NBC affiliate in San Luis Obispo. This station provided coverage about the Parkfield prediction and earthquakes from the time the Parkfield forecast was first issued. It presented programs on the prediction, the science of earthquake prediction, and historical Parkfield earthquakes. Additionally, stories such as these were frequently repeated. In the month of February 1988, there was a month-long series was covered in the evening news entitled "Project Earthquake," with the prediction worked in.

The San Luis Obispo County Office of Emergency Services directed a poster and flyer campaign and conducted radio interviews to increase earthquake risk awareness in the area. Additionally, the American Red Cross conducted training for earthquake disasters and gave many presentations to community groups, school classes, and associations.

Paso Robles public schools also worked hard to prepare for the impending Parkfield quake. They collected and disseminated to staff and students materials from the American Red Cross, an earthquake preparedness workbook, California pamphlets about emergency readiness, brochures from the Federal Emergency Management Agency, and County Office of Emergency Services materials. Schools in Paso Robles hold earthquake drills and larger-scale earthquake exercises annually. Schoolchildren in the area receive material and basic instructions on how to behave during and after earthquakes. Yogi Bear comic books describing the earthquake risk and what people should do about it are easily found in Paso Robles.

Taft

Taft, another community at risk for the Parkfield earthquake, is about 40 miles southwest of Bakersfield, the Kern county seat, and 75 miles from Parkfield. The city has a population of approximately 6,250 and lies in the heart of one of the nation's largest oil-producing regions. The city slogan is "Helping Supply America's Energy Through Petroleum." At 1,000 feet in elevation, Taft boasts of being above the "fog belt" and of being smog free. Oil is Taft's principle industry. Large gushers began coming in on the Midway Sunset Field southeast of Taft in 1910, the same year the city was incorporated. The U.S. Naval Oil reserve is about six miles from Taft and has an estimated production potential of about 200,000 barrels a day. With the 1980s decline in the oil industry accompanied by cuts in oil company crews, Taft's population has declined and its age composition has shifted to a preponderance of older citizens.

Taft residents are concerned about attracting new industry to their community and, not surprisingly, earthquake risk is not advertised in publications about their city. Nevertheless, the same earthquake information sources that existed in other communities at risk for the next Parkfield earthquake also exist in Taft. For example, newspapers, broadcast media, official drills, training, exercises, community action programs, brochures, and coloring and comic books for children have exposed the citizens of Taft to their earthquake risk. Several articles and editorials pertaining to earthquakes and the earthquake prediction have been available in newspapers read by residents of Taft. Served by Bakersfield's television programming, Taft has been exposed to probably more extensive coverage on earthquakes, earthquake response, and the

Parkfield prediction than any other community exposed to risk from the impending Parkfield earthquake.

Although Taft was notable for its relative lack of newspaper information about earthquakes and the Parkfield forecast during the four to five year period after the forecast emerged, it was exposed to extensive coverage on earthquake, earthquake response, and the Parkfield forecast from an award-winning television station out of Bakersfield. The station carried a week of earthquake coverage on the evening news on the first anniversary of the Coalinga quake (May 1-7, 1984). Among other topics, this coverage included the 1952 Bakersfield earthquake. The series ended with a general town meeting in Taft at which multiple pamphlets on earthquake preparedness were handed out to attendees. Subsequent earthquake information was available to Taft residents from extensive coverage over television. This included coverage on the Coalinga earthquake, the Palm Springs earthquake in April 1986, the Whittier-Narrows earthquake in October 1987, information about the Parkfield experiment broadcast during November 1987, and continued coverage of the Parkfield prediction experiment.

The city of Taft has identified all of its hazardous buildings located within the city limits. City officials personally warned the owners and occupants of those buildings about the earthquake risk they face. The Taft schools have undertaken extensive preparations for the next Parkfield earthquake, including quarterly exercise drills for their elementary pupils. In direct response to the Parkfield forecast, schools provided brochures to their students to take home about earthquake readiness. Additionally, the Kern County public schools hold earthquake prediction exercises once a month. The American Red Cross in Taft met with city officials, the police and fire departments, and members of the public to discuss earthquake preparedness because of the forecast. They also made multiple presentations, gave out brochures, and provided training regarding first aid and disaster preparedness to many interested groups after the prediction was announced. These groups included churches, the Girl Scouts, the Boy Scouts, utility companies, and many others.

The State Office of Emergency Services offered suggestions to the city staff members about how to respond to the next Parkfield earthquake and its short-term prediction should one be issued. The city staff prepared a slide show and gave presentations about the Parkfield prediction and earthquake preparedness to many service organizations, the commercial sector, the local college, and other groups and organizations.

Since the Parkfield prediction was officially announced in early 1985 all three communities, Coalinga, Paso Robles, and Taft, have been awash in a virtual stream of information about earthquake risks and about what to do to get ready. The Parkfield earthquake prediction is the first prediction in the history of the United States to be legitimated by the National and California Earthquake Prediction Evaluation Councils. In essence, the call for the development of earthquake prediction technology that emerged out of our nation's examination of the 1964 Alaskan Good Friday earthquake—and the long road traversed from then through 1977 to shepherd in a national earthquake policy that includes the quest for prediction—has resulted in the Parkfield earthquake prediction and warning as its first official prediction product. The next chapter reviews public response to the this earthquake warning by reporting on what the citizens of Coalinga, Paso Robles, and Taft thought and did because of Parkfield earthquake prediction and why. In many ways, the next chapter answers the public policy question "Has the effort put into earthquake prediction in the United States since 1964 at President Johnson's instigation been worth the trouble?"

6

Public Reaction to the Prediction

Study Methods

The publicity that surrounded the Parkfield earthquake prediction exposed the public to information about the prediction, the characteristics of the predicted quake itself, the scientific experiments going on in the area, and what to do to get ready. Information came from official and unofficial sources, it came from all forms of media, schools, special town meetings, all levels of government, and other sources. Because people in the communities at risk, for example, in Taft, Coalinga and Paso Robles, had been exposed to the prediction and its associated warnings, there existed a golden opportunity to study the effects of the prediction/warning. Specifically, researchers wanted to know the extent to which people had heard of the prediction, whether the prediction changed the way that residents perceived their risk for earthquakes, what people remembered about the specifics of the prediction and how to prepare for the quake, people's preferences for future predictions based on their Parkfield experience, and what people had done. Finally, and most important, it was hoped that the findings could inform future attempts to communicate earthquake risk and predictions to the American public.

The state prediction brochure, which was mailed to people's homes, provided a unique research opportunity for several reasons. First, the contents of the brochure clearly revealed the scientific credibility of the prediction. It was noted in the brochure that NEPEC and CEPEC had both approved the forecast, which specifically indicated the important prediction characteristics of time, place, magnitude, and probability. It would therefore be possible to assess the effectiveness of the first quake prediction to emerge from national policy in order to develop predictions in concert with the directives set forth in the National Earthquake Hazards Reduction Program and its amendments.

Second, the brochure was not a one-shot communication, warning, or education event, since it became part of an ongoing and elaborate public information campaign. This enabled systematic study of the long-term character of risk communication as it works in the real world. Finally, the contents of the brochure and other communications about the prediction were sufficiently diverse in type and content to cover all the factors that prior research has documented as important to take into account in order to explain how people perceive and respond to risk information.

For example, there was wide variation in information source, consistency, accuracy, clarity, certainty, guidance about what to do, risk location, communication channel, and frequency (or repetition in the number of times that people heard something on the topic). Variation in these factors guaranteed that the researchers would be well informed and that the study would be based on sound theory.

The research methods used to conduct the study and analyze the data are explained in Appendix B. There were five steps: First, residents of three communities were selected to study; in essence this means that the study was done three times. This allowed determination of whether distance from the predicted quake's epicenter (Taft was far away and Paso Robles and Coalinga were closest) and experience with past quakes (Taft and Paso Robles had no recent damaging earthquakes; Coalinga experienced a bad quake in 1983) revealed how and why people reacted to the Parkfield prediction. Second, researchers visited the three communities and talked with officials in government, schools, the media, the local chapters of the Red Cross, utility companies, and other organizations to learn about all the information to which the people had been exposed. These field investigations ensured that residents would be asked informed questions about all the things that they may have heard. Third, statistically valid samples of households were selected for study in each of the three communities. This allowed for generalizing our findings to everyone who lives in Coalinga, Paso Robles, and Taft on the basis of what was learned from the people included in the study. Fourth, questionnaires were mailed to the homes of the people selected to be in the study. Initially respondents were sent a postcard to inform them of the study and announce that they had been selected as participants; subsequently they were sent a questionnaire. These initial mailings were followed up with additional ones to encourage nonparticipants to fill out the questionnaires. Last, the answers that people gave on the questionnaires were subjected to diverse statistical tests.

Study Findings

Hearing About the Prediction

A variety of communication channels were effective in informing the residents of Coalinga, Paso Robles, and Taft about the prediction. For example, people were exposed through informal word-of-mouth avenues and formal mass media communication channels such as radio, television, and newspapers. Additionally, a variety of different kinds of people used these channels of communication to reach the residents. These included government officials, scientists, emergency management personnel, and news reporters. Most residents heard about the prediction, and most of them heard about it many times and from many different sources. The proportion of respondents who heard about the prediction in each of the communities ranged from 94% in Coalinga and 89% in Paso Robles to 65% in Taft.

Each of the different types of information vehicles reached a substantial portion of the people in each of the communities. Two were the most effective: government organizations such as the California Governor's Office of Emergency Services with its home-mailed brochure, and the newspapers. Printed material, including the brochure, reached the largest number of residents (82% in Coalinga, 71% in Paso Robles, and 49% in Taft). After the brochure, newspapers and television were the most effective channels for communication with the public. Radio was the least effective way to reach the at-risk populations; for example, it reached only 13% of Taft residents.

The brochure was effective perhaps because people tended to keep it and to return to it over and over again, and because it was highly understandable. Although some respondents did not even remember getting the brochure (this ranged from 28% in Coalinga and 38% in Paso Robles to 49% in Taft), more than 85% of the respondents who recalled receiving the brochure reported that it could be readily understood.

Printed materials that were delivered to homes (the brochure and newspapers) were clearly the most effective way to communicate risk and advice to the citizens. Past research on communicating short-term warnings to people only a few hours to a few days before disaster strikes holds that the electronic media, specifically television, are the most effective at reaching the public in short-term warning circumstances (Mileti and Sorensen 1990). That the best way to reach the public about longer-term risks is through printed materials delivered to homes confirms the findings of some other past research on longer-term earthquake prediction situations (Mileti, Hutton, and Sorensen 1981; Turner *et al.* 1984).

The printed word should play a central role in future efforts to inform and educate American populations about not-so-immediate earthquake risks. It is the most effective way, despite the popular notion that television is our basic communication vehicle.

The Risk People Perceived

The public's perception of earthquake risk changed in a way that was almost identical for the citizens in each of the three communities studied. People perceived greater risk of experiencing physical harm and economic losses from a quake in their immediate future—the time period for the predicted quake—than they perceived for any other point in the rest of their lifetimes (see Table 6.1). For example, more respondents in all three communities believed that they or family members would be affected by the Parkfield earthquake in the next few years (53% in Coalinga, 43% in Paso Robles, and 44% in Taft) than perceived comparable risk for any other earthquake at any other time during the rest of their lives (38% in Coalinga, 38% in Paso Robles, and 36% in Taft). These data suggest that roughly half of the people in all three communities actually personalized future near-term losses from the anticipated quake.

These findings are the exact opposite of how the American public typically views the risk of future earthquakes. Almost invariably (as discussed in Chapter 3), people tend to admit only to nonpersonalized quake risk in the distant future, and very few ever actually believe that they will experience quake losses in the short run or in the immediate future (Mileti, Hutton, and Sorensen 1981). The Parkfield earthquake prediction and public information about it apparently helped the public to stop postponing perceived earthquake risk and to stop pushing such risk out into the future; most came to accept it in the nearer-term. In fact, very few people reported (see Table 6.1) that they believed they would not experience the predicted quake in the next few years (14% in Coalinga, 22% in Paso Robles, and 20% in Taft). The prediction also convinced about half of the population that they would soon experience losses in the quake. No official earthquake education effort prior to the Parkfield prediction has achieved this sort of outcome. But what social psychological mechanism led people to those altered perceptions of risk?

The Path of Least Resistance

The residents of Coalinga, Paso Robles, and Taft remembered the Parkfield earthquake prediction. But, they were very selective about what they were able to recall about its parameters, recommendations about protective actions they could take to get ready, and the actual actions they took to get ready.

In general, people remembered and did things along a path of least resistance. People tended to remember and take actions that could be done quickly and inexpensively and to forget about and be less likely to perform actions that were more burdensome.

Table 6.1   Perception of Parkfield and General Earthquake Risk for Each Study
Community (in percentages)

Perceptions	Coalinga	Paso Robles	Taft
I don't believe that I will experience the Parkfield earthquake	13.5	22.1	19.9
I don't believe that I will experience an earthquake	11.1	23.1	17.7
In my lifetime I or someone in my family will experience the Parkfield quake and it will cause physical harm and/or economic losses	33.9	36.3	35.9
In my lifetime I or someone in my family will experience a quake and it will cause physical harm and/or economic losses	37.3	37.9	36.3
In the next few years I or someone in my family will experience the Parkfield quake and it will cause physical harm and/or economic losses	52.7	42.5	44.3
In the next few years I or someone in my family will experience a quake and it will cause physical harm and/or economic losses	51.6	39.0	46.0

What People Remembered

Some of the people in each of the communities we studied did accurately recall the basic prediction elements contained in the brochure (i.e., magnitude, probability, time, potential damage, and ability to feel the quake); more people could not accurately recall them (see Table 6.2).

Table 6.2 Recall of the Prediction's Parameters and the 72-Hour Warning for Each Study Community (in percentages)

Prediction Items Recalled	Coalinga	Paso Robles	Taft
No magnitudes were recalled	29.1	32.8	53.0
Either magnitude 6 or 7	36.5	36.1	27.4
Both magnitudes 6 and 7	34.3	31.1	19.7
No damage parameters recalled	50.1	58.8	72.2
Damage for 6 or 7 magnitudes	27.9	23.3	14.5
Damage for both magnitudes	21.9	17.9	13.2
No felt parameters recalled	19.9	21.0	43.6
One felt parameter recalled	37.7	41.8	27.3
Both felt parameters recalled	42.4	37.3	29.1
No probabilities recalled	45.5	49.3	69.2
Either magnitude 6 with 90% probability or magnitude 7 with 10% probability	30.2	28.9	15.8
Both magnitude 6 & 7 probabilities	24.2	21.8	15.0
Time window not recalled	55.3	60.5	77.4
It will happen by 1993	44.7	39.5	22.5
72-hour warning may be issued	58.2	53.2	37.2
72-hour warning issued by local and state officials	43.5	36.7	29.5
Warning to be given by the media	52.4	47.9	37.6
Telephone hotline number given	30.0	28.3	20.9
Warning followed by other information over the same channels	43.5	46.2	34.2
Several 72-hour warnings may be issued	39.2	34.2	24.8
Warning likely to be canceled within 72-hours if quake doesn't occur	35.4	33.6	24.8

For example, about a third or fewer of our respondents accurately recalled that the prediction stated that the quake could be either a magnitude 6.0 or 7.0: Thirty-four percent of the people in Coalinga, 31% of Paso Robles residents, and 20% of Taft citizens accurately recalled the prediction's statements about magnitude. About a fifth or fewer (22% in Coalinga, 18% in Paso Robles, and 13% in Taft) were able to recall accurately what was said about the earthquake's damage potential. In general, people were better able to recall that the earthquake would be felt in their community. But more people recalled this parameter inaccurately than accurately (42% of Coalinga respondents, 37% in Paso Robles, and 29% in Taft). Recalling the probability and time-window characteristics of the predicted quake was equally difficult for the public. Those who recalled probabilities accurately constituted 24% of the respondents in Coalinga, 22% in Paso Robles, and 15% in Taft. Accurate recollections of the time window for the predicted quake were provided by only 45% of Coalinga residents, 49% of the people in Paso Robles and 23% in Taft.

The public's ability to recall the possible short-term warning that could be issued 72 hours before the predicted quake followed the same pattern as that just described. Public recollections of this prediction parameter ranged from 20% to 60% depending on the specific detail and the community (see Table 6.2). The short-term warning parameters most frequently recalled, and perhaps the most important, were that the public might receive a 72-hour warning and that the warning would be delivered over the broadcast media. The least likely recalled were that there would be a public information hotline and that the warning would be canceled if the earthquake did not strike after 72 hours. As was the case with other findings presented thus far, Coalinga residents recalled more accurately than did people in Paso Robles, and Taft residents were the least likely to remember accurately.

Why would people do things to get ready if they were unable to remember specifics about why they were doing them? Statistical analyses (see Appendixes B and C) and some speculative thinking suggest an explanation.

People may not have thought about the risk of the next Parkfield earthquake in terms of probabilities or in terms of the prediction parameters that concern scientists. Instead, the public may have simply dichotomized the risk. They heard the specifics and they read about them in the OES brochure, but then they made a decision about whether the quake was reason for personal concern. People simply had no reason to remember all the scientific specifics if they already had come to believe that the next Parkfield quake was reason for concern and something for which they should get ready.

Respondents were asked about the preparedness advice they could have received, specifically about the suggestions contained in the brochure distributed by the state OES. Specific guidance recommendations were recalled in an almost identical pattern across the three study communities (see Table 6.3). People were most likely to recall guidance about what to do during the earthquake (e.g., get under a table or desk) and how to prepare for an earthquake disaster, for example, have a flashlight and radio ready.

Table 6.3   Recall of the Preparedness Guidance Offered in the Brochure for Each Study Community (in percentages)

Preparedness Guidance Item Recalled	Coalinga	Paso Robles	Taft
Store food and water	81.6	81.0	60.7
Learn first aid	70.6	65.8	56.0
Have first aid kit available	78.7	77.9	59.0
Keep an emergency supply of needed medications	68.3	67.2	52.6
Develop a family emergency plan	76.7	73.7	56.4
If indoors during an earthquake, stay indoors	76.9	73.7	56.4
Get under table or desk when an earthquake occurs	83.0	81.0	60.3
If outdoors during an earthquake, get to a clear area	85.0	81.8	62.0
Have a flashlight ready	84.4	79.8	61.1
Have a portable radio available	81.0	80.4	58.1
Have heavy gloves and a crescent wrench available	68.0	63.0	50.0
Turn off utilities after a quake	85.0	76.2	60.3
Hang up phone after an earthquake	59.4	51.8	41.5
Only use phone for emergencies after an earthquake occurs	72.3	67.8	55.1
Learn how to prevent fires	57.9	54.3	42.3
Have a fire extinguisher handy	72.6	70.0	53.8
Don't use vehicles unless for emergencies	60.5	57.1	45.3
Form neighborhood quake watch groups	51.9	41.7	29.5
Study work place quake plans	58.2	52.4	39.7
Study school quake plans	62.5	51.8	40.6

People were least likely to recall guidance about preparatory actions that would require extra time and energy to perform, for example, forming a neighborhood watch group and learning the emergency plans at school and work. People in Taft were least likely to recall recommendations such as these, Coalinga residents were most likely to recall them, and Paso Robles residents fell in between.

Community respondents were asked whether they recalled receiving any guidance about what to do to mitigate future earthquake losses. This was in reference to each of the six mitigation guidance recommendations listed in the OES prediction brochure (see Table 6.4).

Table 6.4   Recall of the Mitigation Guidance Offered in the Brochure for Each Study Community (in percentages)

Mitigation Guidance Item Recalled	Coalinga	Paso Robles	Taft
Move heavy objects off high shelves	70.6	66.1	47.9
Anchor house to its foundation	60.5	43.4	34.2
Buy earthquake insurance	65.7	47.1	30.5
Strap down water heater	72.3	55.2	44.0
Protect dishes and glassware	66.0	52.4	39.3
Secure heavy furniture	60.8	49.6	40.2

Ability to recall specific mitigation recommendations ranged from about one-third to three-quarters of the respondents in the study communities, depending on the specific recommendation and the community. In general, the more costly the mitigation recommendations and the more time they would take, the less likely they were recalled. For example, anchoring the house to its foundation and buying earthquake insurance (comparatively more costly recommendations) were remembered by fewer respondents than were less expensive easier recommendations (like moving heavy objects off high shelves, strapping the water heater, and protecting dishes and glassware). Once again, more Coalinga respondents had accurate recollections than did people in Paso Robles, and Taft respondents had the least accurate recollections.

What People Did to Get Ready

When asked what they had actually done to get ready for the predicted Parkfield quake, people answered that they embarked on a massive personal search for additional information about the science of earthquake prediction and for more guidance about the mitigation and preparedness actions that they could take. In general, they did things to get ready that could be done quickly and relatively inexpensively (see Table 6.5).

Around 75% of the people in the three communities sought prediction-science information, and about half sought information on actions to reduce their risk. People searched for more information about the science of earthquake prediction by talking to friends and acquaintances (55% in Coalinga, 52% in Paso Robles, and 46% in Taft) who were easily accessible, and also by finding additional pamphlets and other forms of information from government and nongovernment sources.

Table 6.5 Readiness Actions Performed in Each Study Community Since First Hearing About the Parkfield Earthquake Prediction (in percentages)

Readiness Actions Performed	Coalinga	Paso Robles	Taft
Sought information about quake prediction science from government sources	21.0	18.5	13.2
Sought information about quake prediction science from nongovernment sources	13.5	13.2	13.7
Talked with others about earthquake predictions	55.3	51.8	46.2
Sought information about earthquake readiness from government sources	10.1	15.4	9.4
Sought information about earthquake readiness from nongovernment sources	7.5	12.3	9.0
Talked with others about earthquake readiness	26.9	28.0	27.8
Stockpiled emergency supplies	19.9	27.5	24.4
Developed family emergency plan	10.4	14.3	12.4
Formed an earthquake watch group	3.2	1.1	0.9
Found out what to do during earthquakes	24.8	30.5	27.8
Learned first aid	9.8	6.4	9.0
Bought earthquake insurance	19.6	9.8	10.7
Canceled or delayed large purchases &/or investments	2.6	2.8	2.2
Saved more money	3.2	2.8	6.0
Rearranged household items	22.5	15.1	13.2
Made house more earthquake resistant	17.3	10.1	6.4

People were most likely to take actions that were the easiest to perform, for example, learning what to do during an earthquake (25% in Coalinga, 28% in Paso Robles, and 24% in Taft) and stockpiling emergency supplies. People were least likely to take actions that were time- and energy-intensive, for example, developing a family emergency plan or forming a neighborhood watch group (3% in Coalinga and 1% in Paso Robles and in Taft).

The mitigation response most frequently induced by the prediction was rearranging household items. Some 13% to 23% of the people in the three communities studied performed this action. The next most likely mitigation action was protecting the house. The easy way to accomplish this was by writing a check to purchase quake insurance; 10% to 20% of the respondents bought earthquake insurance. The third most likely mitigation action, taken by 7% to 17% of the people, was taking protective measures through more time-consuming actions such as bolting the house to its foundation (17.3% in Coalinga, 10.1% in Paso Robles, and 6.4% in Taft). Few people did things that would have resulted in negative economic community-level prediction impacts, for example, delaying larger purchases or community investments. But a very few people did seek to reduce their possible losses in this way (2.6% in Coalinga, 2.8% in Paso Robles, and 2.2% in Taft).

Maybe people had a tendency to remember and tell about recommendations for the things they did, and not the things they didn't do. Or it may be that the observed patterns reflect a general tendency for people to perform easier more, simpler tasks before tackling those that are more difficult, complex, and expensive. Another explanation may be that the reported actions are a function of time, and at the point of being queried people had not had enough time since hearing of the prediction and receiving the OES brochure to accomplish the more complicated and time-consuming preparedness and mitigation actions.

Additionally, what can be learned from the almost consistent observation that Coalinga residents (followed in descending order by Paso Robles citizens and the people in Taft) heard, perceived, remembered, and did the most. The people in Coalinga had two reasons to pay attention to the prediction and warning (they are close by and recall their recent 1983 quake); the people of Paso Robles had one reason (they too are close to the predicted epicenter), and the people of Taft had no reason. In fact, this very set of hypotheses led to the research in three separate communities in the first place. But another explanation must be added to the obvious. The Parkfield prediction was named just that; people in Coalinga and Paso Robles know they are the closest towns of any appreciable size to Parkfield, and the people of Taft know that they are somewhat far away. The lower relative salience may have resulted from naming the prediction after the very specific geographical location called Parkfield. Perhaps the residents of Taft thought they had little to worry about, since the predicted quake was a problem for Parkfield (and for places close to Parkfield) and not for them. The long-standing tradition in the geosciences to name earthquakes after cities, towns, and villages may not serve the goals of earthquake prediction. Specific geographical names for predictions may constrain risk perception and action in the public who live in other places.

Preferences for Future Predictions

About 75% of respondents indicated that they would like public information regarding future quake predictions to come from government sources (see Table 6.6). Additionally, about half of them would like the information to come as printed matter like the brochure sent directly to their homes. People clearly were happy with the role of scientists in the Parkfield prediction and with the brochure that the Office of Emergency Services had mailed directly to their homes. These preference data were interpreted to mean that the residents of Coalinga, Paso Robles, and Taft recommend that procedures be the same the next time.

Reasons for Public Reaction

The picture drawn so far does not provide any statistically based insights into why people thought what they thought and why they took the actions they did. If people's significantly elevated risk perceptions influenced their actions to get ready for the quake, what mechanism convinced people to personalize short-term quake risk? A set of complicated multivariate statistical techniques was used to analyze data in a way that would allow answers to these questions. These analyses, the data they produced, and the specific conclusions drawn from them are presented in Appendix C.

Table 6.6 Preferences on the Sources and Channels for Receiving Future Earthquake Prediction Information for Each Study Community (in percentages)

Channel & Source Preferences	Coalinga	Paso Robles	Taft
Government organizations	73.1	71.0	69.5
Nongovernment organizations	26.9	28.6	30.5
Other sources	0.0	0.3	0.0
Electronic media (i.e., radio and television)	18.5	22.7	24.8
Print media (i.e., newspapers)	27.2	25.3	24.1
Other print matter (i.e., brochures)	51.0	49.5	48.5
Meetings and/or conversations	3.3	2.4	2.6

What follows here are the general insights that can be confidently drawn from these more detailed analyses; they were carried out for each of the communities examined. The conclusions add much to our basic understanding of how to upgrade public implementation of quake readiness activities in the United States. They may even have wider application to earthquake education beyond the specific area of earthquake prediction. They can facilitate the general implementation objectives of the National Earthquake Hazards Reduction Program. They also have implications for basic social psychological theory.

The strongest finding was that public readiness behavior was the result of a sequential process. All readiness activities were mostly the consequence of people having engaged in their own search for more information. This search was for all sorts of additional pertinent information, but more was going on than just picking up more literature and a few new details. The search actually reflected people's needs to interact with other people and to talk things over. This was the way people formed personal definitions about the risks they faced as individuals and about actions they should perform. The interaction gave meaning to the problem for people, and it defined appropriate courses of personal protective actions. It gave people the foundation they needed before acting.

In this way, people came to "own" their personal ideas about the prediction, their personal risks, and their personal ideas about an appropriate course of action. Motivating people to search and define was the first significant step, but what motivated people to interact and to discover and define ideas as their own?

The motivation evolved over time and was the result of information being heard over and over again from varied sources and over different channels of communication. In other words, information about the prediction and everything associated with it eventually was reinforced enough to motivate people to engage in searching and interaction behavior that then culminated in protective behavior. Another important form of reinforcement came when people observed others doing things to prepare for the quake. Did one type of information work best to reinforce the prediction and other related topics in people's minds? Yes!

The written brochure provided by the Office of Emergency Services was the most significant piece of information that people obtained. It could be returned to over time, and people could use it to evaluate other news—to help them distinguish between rumor and fact. It adhered to good risk communication principles. For example, it presented information that was comprehensive, specific, clear, consistent, credible, and accurate. And it was supplemented by many other public communications that kept coming over time—before, during, and after the brochure was disseminated.

Recommendations

Send the public a comprehensive written brochure and, if there is sufficient funding, mail it to their homes. A written document can be returned to and reread many times as people consider the risk and what steps to take. If the brochure is mailed to citizens' homes, it takes on a more personal character, which helps people to believe that they are at risk. If there is insufficient funding for a mailing, publish the brochure in area newspapers. This will be slightly less personal and successful than a mailed brochure, but it is still in writing and still arrives in a somewhat personal way on people's doorsteps.

The information in the brochure should explain specifically (1) what the risk is; (2) where the quake is going to happen; (3) when it is going to happen; (4) what the effects will be; (5) what people should do before, during, and after the quake; and (6) where to get more information about the risk, the science of prediction, and preparedness and mitigation actions. This information should be as clear and certain as possible, and the brochure should state that it comes from official sources. Government officials were the most credible information source in our study. However, it is also important to recognize that no one information source is credible for everyone. It is best to include in a brochure a list of sources, for example, government officials, scientists, and emergency response organizations that are familiar to the public, such as the Red Cross.

A brochure must be supplemented with additional information. The public needs to get the message from as many different sources and through as many different channels as possible. Alert the media before the brochure is disseminated, and after dissemination to help reinforce the contents of the brochure. Seeing neighbors, friends, and relatives preparing for the earthquake is very useful, so consider visible demonstration projects in communities that are targets for earthquake predictions. These projects will help convince some members of the public to take action themselves.

It is of paramount importance that the public's attention is captured, that people's interest is sparked, and that they begin to consider doing something about the risk. They need to discuss the risk at local organizations, seek out additional information on their own, and talk with their friends and neighbors about it. This process permits them to gather information and form their own ideas about the level of risk they face and what they should do about it. They may need to feel that taking some protective action is their own idea, but information "ownership" takes time. Position supplemental information in the local community for use during this process, such as coloring books, brochures, slide shows, film strips, and additional advice on preparedness and mitigation actions.

The prediction was quite a success (from a public response viewpoint) regardless of whether the predicted earthquake ever happens. The experiment portion of the prediction was designed to further knowledge in the geosciences. The social science experiment allowed by the Parkfield quake prediction has been successful. But the Parkfield earthquake prediction and public response to it is part of an ongoing story about earthquake prediction that began in 1964 with the Good Friday earthquake in Alaska.

7

Present and Future
Predictions

The Parkfield prediction may well be the most studied quake prediction from geological, seismological, and public reaction viewpoints to have ever emerged. It provided physical scientists with the opportunity to experiment with different prediction techniques. It propelled some investigators into national prominence and afforded them an opportunity to be published in leading scientific journals and periodicals. And it certainly produced many new insights about how to manage earthquake prediction information for the public's benefit. The experiment also resulted in a somewhat permanent blending of the physical and social sciences with each other and with the emergency management communities. The experiment resulted in the United States overcoming the parochial boundaries of different professions, disciplines, and sciences to approach earthquake prediction from interdisciplinary and fully informed points of view. This was not a small accomplishment, nor was it an easily won prize. The potential public benefits may someday be enormous.

But a good amount of time has passed since the Parkfield prediction was made, and the earthquake has not yet happened. Many of the leading scientists that gave the experiment life have moved on to other projects in different geographical areas. The experiment has now been left to new-comers, and continued data collection has been handed over to a handful of technicians.

A generation of post-Parkfield "predictions" has emerged, and they illustrate the legacy of Parkfield: The interdisciplinary character of quake prediction that emerged during the first several years of the Parkfield experiment is now somewhat standard national practice. At present, two scientifically credible quake forecasts are in place. Both of them illustrate how the Parkfield experiment has put our nation at the forefront of developing, disseminating, and using earthquake prediction information. The earthquake catastrophes "predicted" for the near-term are hardly reason for enthusiasm, but if they come and if they are preceded by short-term predictions, our nation will likely manage them on the cutting edge using knowledge and cooperation from all applicable fields.

The San Francisco Bay Area

The 1989 Loma Prieta earthquake in the San Francisco Bay area did more than cause damage. It raised concern among members of the scientific community that the probability of subsequent quakes in the area could be substantially changed. The result was that the National Earthquake Prediction Evaluation Council organized a working group to reexamine the probabilities of large earthquakes in the Bay Area. The group sought new interpretations and examined physical changes that resulted from the 1989 Loma Prieta earthquake. The working group was composed of experts from the U.S. Geological Survey, several universities, and the private sector.

The working group issued its report in mid-1990. The probabilities of large earthquakes (magnitude 7.0 or larger) along the San Andreas fault system in northern California were in fact raised above what they had been before the Loma Prieta quake had struck the area. The significant statements about revised probabilities were straightforward.

> We now estimate the chance of one or more large earthquakes in the San Francisco Bay region in the coming 30 years to be about 67 percent. A magnitude 7 or larger earthquake along any of the segments considered by the Working Group will have a major impact on the entire San Francisco Bay region. . . . Estimates of the long-term rates of slip on the San Andreas and Hayward faults are revised upward relative to the previous estimates. A higher slip rate shortens the expected time to the next earthquake and increases the likelihood of an earthquake. The Working Group estimates the slip rate on the San Andreas fault within the San Francisco Bay region to be 19 mm/yr compared to the previous (1988) Working Group estimate of 16 mm/yr. The slip rate on the Hayward fault is now estimated at 9 mm/yr compared to the previous estimate of 7.5 mm/yr (U.S. Geological Survey 1990, p. 1).

The working group also went on to consider the actual impact of the physical characteristics of the Loma Prieta earthquake on future quake risk.

> The probability of an earthquake on the segment where the Loma Prieta earthquake occurred (southern Santa Cruz Mountains segment) is low following that earthquake. Models of crustal deformation indicate that stress increased on nearby segments of the San Andreas fault as a result of the Loma Prieta earthquake. The stress increase shortens the time to the next earthquake on these

segments. However, it is not known if the magnitude of this effect is large enough to be significant (U.S. Geological Survey 1990, p. 2).

The report that the working group prepared was issued as an official U.S. Geological Survey report and was disseminated to the standard sort of people who receive such documents. The next step was seen as carrying the word forward to the members of the public at risk. Peter Ward, a seismologist at the USGS in Menlo Park, California, was given the chore of developing an appropriate mechanism to inform the public.

Developing an Approach to Inform the Public

The results of the research performed on the societal response aspects of the Parkfield earthquake prediction were not unknown to members of the USGS, to other members of the working group, and to earthquake management officials in California. They recalled that prediction information was found to help the public better perceive risk and prepare for future earthquakes in areas at risk for the Parkfield quake, and they sought to learn more about this process. An elaborate effort was initiated by seismologists to contact social scientists and emergency management officials in an effort to gain their recommendations about how to best inform the public in the Bay Area about the revised quake probabilities following Loma Prieta.

The product of this search and interdisciplinary work resulted in many recommendations including the following: First, public risk information would work best if it was written and distributed in the form of a document like a brochure. Second, the distribution of a written document should be preceded and followed by other media accounts of it to heighten and reinforce public interest. Third, the brochure should not come from one source but rather should be attributed to a variety of organizations and groups to increase its credibility to the public. Fourth, the brochure should present a range of topics including where people can get additional information. Finally, the brochure should be written in clear language and emphasize what people should do to get ready.

This very sort of document was developed and disseminated in some 2.4 million Sunday newspapers throughout the Bay Area on September 9, 1990. Stockpiles of other documents were positioned throughout the Bay Area before the brochure was disseminated so that they would be available for members of the public who would request additional information after the brochure was disseminated. Press conferences were scheduled and held before and after the distribution. Millions more copies of the brochure have since been requested by people in California and also in almost every other state in the nation.

The newspaper insert was titled "The Next Big Earthquake in the Bay Area May Come Sooner Than You Think." It was prepared to resemble a magazine. It was printed on slick bond paper and was stapled and folded. Its 10 by 13 inch size and 24-page length contributed to its magazine-like appearance. The magazine insert also made extensive use of color. It was printed in red, green, yellow, blue, and it also had white sections with black lettering. The document was also divided into about a dozen topical sections. The titles of these sections were placed at the top of the pages and they were printed in bold lettering. The insert also contained maps and pictures. For example, the centerfold was a map of the Bay Area that clearly illustrated the location of faults and different ground conditions with different prospects for experiencing damage in a large earthquake. The document was impressive, and its appearance set it apart from the rest of the newspaper, which was printed on pulp.

This insert and the campaign that surrounded its dissemination was much more than simply a distribution of information to the public about future quake risk. It represented, perhaps for the first time in the history of the nation, the cooperation of federal, state, local, and private-sector organizations as well as the blending of social scientific knowledge about communicating risk information to the public with what the physical scientists had to say. It was the first truly interdisciplinary attempt to blend cutting-edge knowledge in all fields to deal with earthquake prediction information. What made it unique was that it happened naturally, as if physical scientists had always conversed with their social scientist counterparts while at the same time taking to heart input from state and local emergency management organizations.

What the Public Was Told

The insert told people how much the ground would likely shake in the next large Bay Area quake. This was done using a multicolored map. The map showed the location of several cities and had colored bars that represented how many more times stronger the next possible quake(s) would be in relation to the Loma Prieta. For example, it told that Santa Rosa will shake 48 times stronger if the next quake happens on the Rogers Creek fault, Oakland will shake 12 times stronger if the quake happens on the northern Hayward fault, Fremont will shake 6 times stronger if it happens on the southern Hayward fault, San Francisco will shake 5 times stronger if it happens on the peninsula segment of the San Andreas, and so on.

The insert went on to describe why experts think that a major quake is highly likely to occur soon. The document stated that it was based on the 1990 working group report issued by the USGS, that that report gave a 67% probability of another quake the size of Loma Prieta or larger in the next 30 years, and that this means that it is now twice as likely to happen as to not happen. The public was told that the Loma Prieta quake increased the odds of another quake and why, and that the next one would likely occur in a much more populated area.

Subsequent information conveyed the idea that there are many actions that members of the public can take to get ready, and people were presented with a variety of recommended actions. These included detailed ideas about appropriate elements to include in an earthquake emergency plan at home, in the neighborhood, at school and at work. And people were advised of the need to store emergency supplies and told how to engage in simple actions that would help protect their belongings.

The insert also explained how people could estimate the actual risk that they faced, for example, how they could determine the safety of their homes, schools, and other buildings that they used, and how they could determine quake risk by location according to factors such as shaking intensity, ground slides and soft soils, and proximity to fault lines. A map was also provided so that members of the public could locate where they lived and worked in relation to particularly hazardous areas.

Information was also presented that helped people understand how to interpret and respond to possible future quake advisories or predictions. Finally, detailed information was given about where interested persons could go or whom they could call to get additional information about a range of specific earthquake and readiness topics.

As might be expected, research is currently under way to determine societal response to the dissemination of public information about the next major Bay Area earthquake. That research is investigating response by the public as well as by governments (city, county, state, and federal) and the private sector. This research is being conducted by social scientists, but it includes input from and was partly shaped by members of local, state, and federal emergency planning organizations and by physical scientists. Apparently, an interdisciplinary feedback loop has developed in the field of quake prediction.

We have come a long way from only a couple of decades ago when physical scientists worked in isolation, local communities were surprised by predictions, and social scientists would arrive on the scene about a year after a prediction to ask people questions. The contemporary interdisciplinary character of earthquake prediction and earthquake prediction management is also illustrated in the most current "prediction" in the nation.

The Southern Section of the San Andreas

The Earthquakes

Southern California was struck by a double earthquake on June 28, 1992. The first of the events happened at 4:58 a.m. PDT; and it was 7.4 magnitude and was centered in the Landers area north of Joshua Tree in the Mojave Desert. The second quake happened three hours later at 8:04 a.m. PDT. It was magnitude 6.5 and happened near Big Bear Lake. Many aftershocks followed in the 4.4 to 5.3 magnitude range.

The governor of California requested that the president declare San Bernardino and Riverside counties as major disaster areas on July 1, 1992, and President Bush signed the declaration the next day. The quakes resulted in 1 death, 25 serious injuries, and 372 other injuries. Losses were estimated at some $74 million in both counties.

The region of these earthquakes has a recent history of seismic activity. Quakes in the area include the 6.5 magnitude Desert Hot Springs earthquake, the 5.2 magnitude Galway quake in 1975, the 1979 Homestead Valley-Johnson Valley 4.9 magnitude earthquake, and the 1986 magnitude 6.1 Palm Springs quake. The region has also seen an increased amount of seismic activity since 1986 including a precursor to the Landers quake. This was the magnitude 6.1 Joshua Tree earthquake that happened on April 22, 1992.

The Landers earthquake's aftershocks extended south to the San Andreas fault, and the Big Bear earthquake's aftershocks extended southwest to the San Andreas fault, where a magnitude 4.4 earthquake occurred near Yucaipa. The 4.4 event was consistent with the type of faulting that has typically occurred on the San Andreas fault. These earthquakes and their aftershocks occurred in close proximity to the section of the San Andreas that has been locked since the last great southern California earthquake, which happened in 1857.

Some aftershocks were large enough to cause additional injuries, for example, a 5.3 magnitude aftershock struck six miles east of Big Bear Lake on July 8, 1992, causing at least 10 people to go the hospital with injuries and 50 more homes to slip off their foundations. The aftershocks were large enough to impose quake damage on an almost daily basis. Accounts of public distress filled most area newspapers as people became weary from ongoing aftershock activity. Reports from Bear Valley Community Hospital revealed that the most widespread problem was mental strain imposed by the aftershocks. The quakes and aftershocks continued. A magnitude 5.1 earthquake struck on July 11, 1992, about 12 miles northeast of Mojave. It was reported to not be in the aftershock zones of either the Landers or the Big Bear earthquakes.

The Emerging Prediction

It is not a surprise that the public, scientists, and governments began to express concern that this series of quakes could be unraveling the seismic knot that had kept the southern section of the San Andreas locked since 1857, and that a great quake might occur soon. News of such concerns among scientists was first made public on July 13, 1992. Leading newspapers in southern California and others such as the *New York Times* carried stories on the private views of leading earthquake scientists. These stories reported that scientists had reviewed preliminary data and were concluding that the Landers and Big Bear earthquakes significantly increased the likelihood that the southern part of the San Andreas fault would soon generate the "Big One." Scientists also suggested that the people who live in southern California should treat the recent series of quakes as a final warning. Dr. Allan Lindh, director of the USGS Seismological Branch in Menlo Park, for example, suggested that "it's time to make the last pass through our cities, homes and lives and act as if the damn thing will happen tomorrow" (*San Bernardino Sun*, July 13, 1992). Dr. Lucille Jones, a leading expert on the southern San Andreas at the USGS office in Pasadena, was quoted as saying that the recent quakes were a wake-up call and that the next great southern California quake could happen as soon as within the next two years.

The news kept coming when on July 16, 1992, the magnitudes of the Landers and Big Bear quakes were revised upward to 7.5 and 6.6, respectively. It was now some three weeks after the Landers quake. The public had felt the quakes and dozens of aftershocks, listened to and read untold numbers of news stories about what they experienced, and heard from some of the nation's leading quake experts about the odds that the Big One was just around the corner. Rumors began to fly among members of what had become a supervigilant public, for example, an underground volcano had erupted and was spewing lava toward the San Andreas fault. And stories also revealed signs of psychosocial stress among members of the victim populations, including depression, nightmares, feelings of going crazy, gastrointestinal sickness, anxiety and others. These symptoms are often found in postdisaster-stricken populations that are undergoing severe anxiety, and some people speculated that the continuing aftershocks were making matters worse.

The number of rumors circulating among members of the affected population continued to grow. For example, on July 20, 1992, the grapevine reported that the California Institute of Technology (Caltech), which houses a major center for seismological research, had ordered its employees to leave town. It was also rumored that the water tables under southern California were dropping and that this was a certain sign that the

Big One was about to strike the area. Over 5,000 aftershocks had been detected up to this point, and some 80 of them were at least 4.0 magnitude.

Concerns among the seismologists also continued. For example, a major expert was quoted in most area newspapers and the *New York Times* as saying that he would not be surprised if a large quake happened on the San Andreas within the next few years. Rumors fed on statements like these, and some believed that a great quake was no more than a few months away. The public began to purchase military surplus supplies, and survival gear and to stockpile food and water.

The fodder of fear and rumor is often based in real events, and the events reported to the public in southern California continued to provide fertile ground. For example, the *Los Angeles Times* reported on July 23, 1992, that the earthquakes had triggered a strange event in Ventura, a county some 100 or so miles away from the epicenters. It was reported that crude oil equivalent to 60 barrels or more had been found in creeks in the Ventura County mountains in the prior two weeks and that authorities thought the seepage was triggered by the recent quakes. The next day the *San Bernardino Sun* carried a story covering some of the economic impacts that would be caused by the Big One. It told of some $40 billion of damage and predicted that some insurance companies would go bankrupt. Aftershocks, damage, and rumors continued into August. The media filled the public mind with accounts of how the seismologists were preparing, for example, by putting film over their homes' windows to keep the glass from shattering and bolting their furniture to the walls. Reports were issued on the safety of some of the area's most important structures. For example, there was a report on how the Seven Oaks Dam in the San Bernardino area would be affected by a great quake.

A peculiar state of affairs existed in southern California as July 1992 turned into August. There was real reason for concern that the odds of a great quake striking the area had gone up and that such a quake could even occur soon. More than a few reputable seismologists were telling the public about this concern, but no scientific basis besides a casual review of the data—let alone a review by either the National or California Earthquake Prediction Evaluation councils—existed for making a prediction. Many aftershocks could be felt by the public, and these served as physical cues that the San Andreas seemed to be awakening. The media reported the opinions of individual seismologists who spoke as if they believed that the Big One was impending. Rumors confirmed the worst fears in some people's minds, and some members of the public were acting as if a great quake had just been predicted for the short term by buying survival equipment and supplies. Their actions were confirmed on November 30, 1992 when a scientific report was issued that set a 47%

probability for a large quake in southern California during the next 5 years. All of these events existed in a historical context. The residents of southern California have been told since 1980 that the odds of experiencing a great quake within the following 30 or so years was fairly high.

The Legacy of the Parkfield Experiment

The series of events that began around the August 1, 1992 revealed the phenomenal societal benefits of the Parkfield earthquake prediction experiment. An interdisciplinary approach was induced and implemented largely under the direction of the state of California through the offices of the state geologist and through Emergency Services. Obvious multidisciplinary and jurisdictional problems and issues existed, including (1) the need for well-informed scientific judgment and consensus about future quake potential—certainly the public interest would be better served if different groups and individuals were not all saying different things; (2) the need for a reasonably well-based comprehensive scientific review of the data regarding future quake risk—scientific judgments about future risk could only be improved if they were based on all relevant information and data; (3) the need to address public concerns, fears, and rumors—the public was reacting to events as if a real prediction had been issued, and this needed to be addressed; (4) the need to take advantage of heightened citizen interest to increase public readiness in the event that a great quake was likely—another damaging quake might happen, and people should be as ready as they could be; (5) the need to coordinate actions by different actors including the California Office of Emergency Services, the Southern California Earthquake Center at the University of Southern California, the U.S. Geological Survey, the Federal Emergency Management Agency, the California and National Earthquake Prediction Evaluation councils—too many cooks can spoil any broth, and it seemed worthwhile to try to put the public interest in front of organizational ones; and (6) the need to involve contributions from different disciplines and perspectives including seismology, public policy, sociology, public relations, and social psychology.

Too many individual scientists were speaking out on the odds that a great quake would likely occur soon on the southern section of the San Andreas without a fully informed scientific basis for the thoughts that they articulated. Concern that some were saying too much too soon was particularly acute among those who observed that the aftershock sequence that followed the Landers and Big Bear quakes resembled typical aftershocks that follow all quakes of the magnitudes of those experienced. The public interpreted what they heard almost as warnings for the Big One, and people were simply scared. Earthquake organizations were also speaking out or getting ready to issue formal statements on the topic, for example, the U.S. Geological Survey, the California Institute of Technology, and the Southern California Earthquake Center at the University of Southern California.

Social scientists had learned that it is easier for the public to understand what scientists try to tell them if those scientists conduct their debates amongst themselves and then go to the public with an accurate account of their consensus, their differences, and the reasons for both. The state of California moved quickly to develop a forum wherein scientists could confer with one another.

Individual organizations were invited to put the public interest first, join in the debate, and participate in a news conference where considered expert opinion would be made public. It was also decided, after elaborate consultation with social scientists, that a press conference/press release format would best inform the public. This format was adopted by members of the seismological community and by emergency managers in the state. It was planned that such news conferences would be held weekly to present the public with the most current and up-to-date information available.

But earthquake predictions and the deliberations of those who discuss and issue them are typically leaked to the press (see, for example, the Kawasaki prediction in the mid-1970s described in Chapter 4). On August 5, 1992, the very day that the first cooperative press conference was to be conducted, the *Orange County Register*, the largest newspaper in that part of southern California, leaked the news that top experts were meeting to formulate a joint statement about the odds of a future great quake. The headline read: "Experts Fear Tremors Point to the Big One."

Worried about public safety, state and federal officials have created a commission to examine how much the two major earthquakes that struck Southern California on June 28 increased the chances of the Big One. . . . The 12-member commission isn't expected to produce a definitive answer, but the board will push scientists to clarify the implications of the 7.5 quake at Landers and subsequent 6.6 temblor at Big Bear. . . . The quakes raised a lot of questions that are still hanging. . . . The commission will try to get some answers. . . . The researchers include Lucy Jones, a U.S. Geological Survey seismologist who says that the twin quakes of June 28 definitely increased the risk that something big will happen on the San Andreas. But we're far from consensus on how much that risk has gone up, or when something is likely to happen (*Orange County Register*, August 5, 1992, p. A3).

State and federal emergency managers and social and physical scientists had also discussed and sought a practical way to deal with the rumors and fears that existed in the public mind. Conflicting information and confusion about risk and what people should do about it had long been shown by social science research to be counterproductive for the public. The state-led plan was to also address public fears and rumors. It was decided that members of some state organizations would monitor the media to detect prevalent rumors and fears. Those issues would then be addressed at the weekly press conferences along with other seismological information, and a rumor-control hot line would be established. The hot line was called the Earthquake Safety Hotline. It was announced on August 5, 1992. The press release that opened the hot line stated the following:

Californians now have a toll-free number to call for accurate earthquake information. A new Earthquake Safety Hotline, 1-800-286-SAFE (1-800-286-7233), puts callers on the line for the latest earthquake news and scientific reports, as well as information that can help them prepare for earthquakes when they do occur. The Hotline will operate Monday through Friday, from 7 a.m. to 7 p.m. Participating in the hotline are state, local, and federal agencies, including the California Office of Emergency Services, U.S. Geological Survey, California Department of Conservation, California Institute of Technology, Federal Emergency Management Agency, Southern California Earthquake Center, and many local government agencies. There have been more than 10,000 aftershocks from the Landers and Big Bear earthquakes of June 28, and numerous calls to dozens of different government agencies and universities from area residents alarmed by a wide range of rumors and uncertainty. "The Earthquake Safety Hotline will provide a central place, a clearing house, for rumor control," says Dr. Richard Andrews, Director of the California Office of Emergency Services. "Callers can speak directly to one of our Resource Technicians, talk about what they've heard, get information on what's really happening, and also ask for literature to help them prepare for earthquakes." Hotline technicians will also be in close communication with scientists and will be able to quickly relay information as it is developed. The Earthquake Safety Hotline has TDD capability for the deaf and hearing-impaired persons, and will also serve callers who speak languages other than English (California Safety Information Center, August 5, 1992, pp. 1-2).

The sequence of events called into action in response to public concerns and fears following the Landers and Big Bear earthquakes was precedent-setting. Cooperation was forthcoming from a range of different government organizations; physical and social scientists worked side by side to manage the events that evolved, drawing upon knowledge from across disciplines; and the state and federal bureaucracies orchestrated one of the most interdisciplinarily informed campaigns to manage a "prediction" ever witnessed.

The events in southern California have not gone away. The panel established to consider how the Landers and Big Bear quakes impact the odds of a great quake in that part of the state are busy doing their work as we write this last chapter. The next critical episode in the history of earthquake prediction may well unfold in southern California over the next few months or years.

The Future

The nation has come a very long way since the great Alaskan earthquake of 1964, when attention was first paid to the science of earthquake prediction, and since the National Earthquake Hazards Reduction Act of 1977 established policy and increased financial support for the development of prediction science. But short-term scientific earthquake prediction is still in the realm of science fiction rather than scientific fact. The effort has not been in vain or wasted. Our nation is now able to benefit from long-term quake forecasts in the form of earthquake probabilities, for example, like those now in place for the San Francisco Bay Area following the 1989 Loma Prieta earthquake. These sorts of forecasts may not be analogous to predictions and warnings for other natural hazards such as hurricanes, but they do hold great benefit. For example, they are a basis for expanding the use of special techniques to increase quake safety, including building codes and practices and land use regulation. Short-term earthquake predictions—based on scientific theory rather than on changes in statistical probabilities—that foretell disastrous earthquakes a few days away continue to elude the physical scientists who must do their research in a human time frame on a problem that exists in geological time.

But our nation has made phenomenal strides in readying for societal prediction response and management. We lead the world in cataloging public response and risk communication lessons to implement should a prediction ever emerge. We are also at the forefront of integrating useful knowledge from across disparate disciplines and professions. Earthquake prediction may be at the forefront of science and public management in terms of the lessons learned and used to blend theory and practice.

Epilogue

The development of earthquake prediction technologies is a continuing process in the United States. Accompanying the development of the technology to predict quakes are developments in communicating earthquake risks to the public. These two areas of expertise go hand in hand. Progress in predicting quakes leads to progress in communicating predictions to the public. Until very recently, however, official announcements of earthquake predictions were primarily for those of a long-term nature. No short-term earthquake predictions had ever been officially sanctioned in the United States by either the National or California Earthquake Prediction Evaluation Councils. In the midst of this book's being prepared for publication, this circumstance changed. With a recent development, officially approved short-term prediction of earthquakes can now be said to have moved from the realm of fiction to the realm of fact.

The Parkfield earthquake prediction experiment has been on the forefront of both the development of earthquake prediction technology and the effective communication of those developments to the public. The Parkfield experiment represents a continuing chronicle of earthquake prediction efforts and events surrounding those efforts. In October, 1992, yet another chapter in the life of the Parkfield Experiment unfolded.

On October 19, 1992, Parkfield became known as the sight of the first official NEPEC/CEPEC short-term earthquake prediction specifying time, place, and magnitude of occurrence to emerge in the United States. This prediction led the California to issue its highest type of earthquake warning, a level A alert, to members of the public residing in the region of central California surrounding Parkfield.

This A alert was triggered when the USGS picked up seismic readings of a 4.7 magnitude earthquake under Middle Mountain, just north of Parkfield, late in the evening of October 19. An earthquake of this approximate size had been predetermined to be a prime signal that the "characteristic" (5.5 to 6.0 magnitude) or potentially larger (7.0 magnitude) Parkfield quake was imminent. Notification of this short-term prediction was sent almost immediately, in the form of a warning from the state Office of Emergency Services, to local jurisdictions in the seven-county region composing the Parkfield area of risk.

The warning indicated that the Parkfield earthquake had a significantly increased likelihood of occurring within a 72-hour period of release of the notice. The likelihood of occurrence was stated as 37% or greater. But as time passed, this likelihood diminished. And by morning of the third day of the warning period, the chances of the Parkfield quake occurring had decreased to about 5%. Late in the evening of this third day, the alert expired and the earthquake's likelihood of occurrence reverted back to less than a 2.8% chance on any given day.

Even though this prediction went unfulfilled, it presented a good opportunity to study social reaction to the first real-life, NEPEC/CEPEC approved, short-term earthquake warning in the country. With a quick-response research grant from the Natural Hazards Research and Applications Information Center at the University of Colorado in Boulder, sociologists from the Hazards Assessment Laboratory at Colorado State University conducted a case study of this distinctive event. Following are the highlights of findings, interpretations and impressions of public reaction (for a more detailed account see Fitzpatrick and O'Brien 1992) derived from this effort to contribute to the developing body of knowledge on social response to earthquake predictions.

Members of the public could hardly escape hearing about this short-term prediction. The public principally heard about it through the news media, which served as the vehicle for getting word of the alert to the public. And both print and electronic media did a very thorough job. The media made the alert a very prominent issue—it was front-page news or the lead story for three days. Members of the media from across the state hurried to interview seismologists, state officials, and residents in the Parkfield area. And while waiting for the earthquake to happen, news reporters scripted stories that exhaustively and repetitiously detailed the prediction. But hearing about the alert, in all of its detail, did not necessarily mean that the public perceived the alert as defining a personally imminent earthquake threat. Nor did it mean that the public engaged in wholesale readiness behavior.

The consistent message, unremittently delivered to the public, was that the predicted earthquake had a 37% or greater likelihood of occurrence within a three-day period. But members of the public did not necessarily take this to mean that they were personally at increased risk. More than anything else, probability statements were likely taken to mean that the scientists predicting the quake were uncertain that it would actually occur. This is not surprising, since research on public reaction to the Parkfield prediction experiment (see Chapter 6) revealed that people tend to dichotomize risk. That is, they preferred to define the Parkfield quake as something that would or would not affect their lives. During this short-term situation, we observed this same dichotomizing tendency. People's inclinations to define the warning as meaningful or not meaningful were not based on stated likelihoods of occurrence but were rooted in past experiences with damaging earthquakes and with feeling the precursor quake leading up to the official warning. While feeling the precursor may have served to reinforce the warning the alert message was intended to convey, people were likely to use the probability statements issued in the alert more as a way of defining the scientists' sense of inaccuracy and uncertainty than as a way to define their own personal risk. The precise probability statements may have been confusing to the public and may have helped some people decide that they were not at risk when they were actually at increased risk.

Nevertheless, for the most part, the public felt scientists had attempted honestly and sincerely to make a short-term prediction for the Parkfield quake and to share with the public increased concerns about the quake's occurring. If nothing else, the alert served to remind the public that they are at continuing risk from earthquakes and raised the salience of earthquake vulnerability in the mind of the public, at least during the short run of the warning period. The alert also provided a good opportunity to circulate information about readiness actions the public could take to become better prepared for inevitable future earthquakes. And in some ways, this short-term prediction may have served to infuse a much-needed sense of life back into the Parkfield experiment.

Even though people generally perceived the alert as real and credible, they did not allow such perceptions to disrupt daily routines to any significant degree. The public did engage in some readiness activities in anticipation of the quake, but the reasons given for taking these actions did not reflect responses to the alert so much as they reflected other factors. The two principal factors related to response were experience with damaging earthquakes (i.e., the devastating earthquake of 1983 in Coalinga) and whether the 4.7 magnitude precursor quake was felt. Many members of the public also engaged in efforts to get more information about the alert. This was evidenced by inquiries to county offices of emergency services and the recently instituted state earthquake hot line concerning the alert's meaning and what should be done about it.

Readiness activities in which the public engaged consisted mostly of doing things that could be readily accomplished and that were easily affordable. People purchased bottled water and fresh batteries more often than they prepared in any other way. The removal of pictures and mirrors from walls, and the securing of objects that could fall or be thrown around during an earthquake were also accomplished to some degree.

Although readiness actions were not performed in a broad and sweeping manner throughout the area, clearly the circumstances surrounding the alert did induce more readiness activity than might have otherwise been accomplished. The alert also certainly reminded people of their earthquake risk. Nevertheless, questions remain about the public's ability to instill readiness behaviors into its cultural fabric as a way to minimize damages from earthquakes.

Impressions derived from this case study strongly suggest that most of central California possesses only a modest earthquake culture. The precursor quake was a reminder from Mother Nature that her inhabitants continue to be at risk. The A alert was the vehicle by which the state communicated Mother Nature's warning to the public. This exceptional alert amounted to but one more gear in developing a machine to sew threads of earthquake salience and readiness into the social fabric of central California. More than anything else, the alert served as a reminder to Californians that they live under a great earthquake threat. And in so doing, it provided people with a much-needed stimulus to take stock of their earthquake readiness capabilities.

Residents throughout central California are well aware that they live in earthquake territory. Such awareness, however, has not yet moved people to the point of fully developing an earthquake culture. Moving earthquake awareness to a level at which readiness actions become part of the cultural fabric of this society remains problematic. Perhaps it is to be expected that when a public constantly lives under the threat of natural events, which are largely unpredictable and without season, that it will become complacent and fatalistic. But such a state of affairs does not mean that a complacent and fatalistic cultural condition should remain the status quo. Central California is the center of the most renowned earthquake prediction experiment in the world. It is likely steeped in more information about earthquake risk and what to do to get ready than most places on earth. This region also well illustrates the need, for government and other players, to relentlessly pursue efforts to sew readiness behaviors into the cultural fabric of earthquake-threatened areas throughout the United States.

Appendix A

Public Announcement:
Studies Forecasting Moderate
Earthquake Near Parkfield, California,
Receive Official Endorsement

The forecast that an earthquake of magnitude 5.5 to 6.0 is likely to occur in the Parkfield, Calif., area within the next several years (1985-1993) has been reviewed and accepted by State and Federal evaluation panels according to an announcement today (April 5, 1985) by the U.S. Geological Survey.

A letter summarizing the results of the scientific review of the Parkfield forecast was sent to Mr. William Medigovich, Director of the California Office of Emergency Services, by Dr. Dallas Peck, Director of the U.S. Geological Survey.

Parkfield has been the site of a U.S.G.S. earthquake prediction experiment that is using sophisticated distance measuring devices and other monitoring equipment in an attempt to determine and monitor signals that might presage an earthquake. The research that led to today's statement has been carried out by William H. Bakun and Allen G. Lindh of the U.S. Geological Survey and Thomas B. McEvilly of the University of California. Their conclusions are based on analyses of reports of earthquakes in the Parkfield area in 1857, 1881, and 1901 and seismograph records of events near Parkfield in 1922, 1935, and 1966. The average interval between these events is 22 years and statistical analyses indicate a high probability (over 90%) of another earthquake in the region within the 1985 to 1993 interval. The seismograph records of the last three Parkfield earthquakes are very similar, leading to the hypothesis of a characteristic earthquake in the Parkfield region of about magnitude 6 on the Richter scale.

Parkfield lies along the San Andreas fault in a sparsely populated region about 170 miles south of San Francisco and 180 miles north of Los Angeles. An earthquake of magnitude 6 is of moderate size, at the threshold of being able to cause moderate damage to some structures that have not been designed for earthquake resistance.

The last Characteristic Parkfield Earthquake occurred on June 28, 1966, registered a magnitude slightly less than 6, and caused only minor damage to wood-frame houses in the region.

The results of the Parkfield study by Bakun, Lindh, and McEvilly have recently been evaluated and endorsed by the National Earthquake Prediction Evaluation Council and the California Earthquake Prediction Evaluation Council. These bodies advise federal and state officials respectively on the validity of statements and studies regarding the occurrence of future earthquakes. The National Council concluded that the findings at Parkfield constitute a long-term prediction, a term adopted by both councils to describe a statement on the occurrence of an earthquake at a specific place and within a time interval of a few years to a few decades.

In their evaluation of the research, the two prediction review panels said that the potential exists for the next earthquake in the Parkfield region to be larger than the 1966 shock, and for the fault rupture to extend southeast into the adjacent 25-mile segment of the San Andreas fault. Both panels agreed, however, that the evidence for this larger earthquake was speculative and required additional data in review.

Under a program of earthquake prediction research, the U.S. Geological Survey maintains an array of sensitive geophysical monitoring instruments in the Parkfield region in an attempt to predict the occurrence of the expected earthquake more precisely. The California Division of Mines and Geology also maintains a large number of instruments to measure the effects of the earthquake.

The California Office of Emergency Services has reviewed the evaluation with local officials and will take coordinated action should the extensive monitoring equipment arrayed throughout the Parkfield region indicate that the anticipated earthquake is imminent.

U.S. Geological Survey
Office of the Director

Appendix B

Methods Used in the Research

Because each study community was in the "area at risk" for the next Parkfield earthquake, each sampling, data collection, and analysis method used in this study was repeated three times. This appendix describes the methodological decisions and approaches employed.

Discussed are the quasi-experimental field design, how communities were selected for study, the qualitative field research, the cross-sectional surveys of community populations, how data were collected, how the study's concepts were measured to enable hypothesis testing, the descriptive statistical analysis of the survey data employed, and the hypothesis-testing and path-modeling techniques utilized to explain social action. Obviously, a range of social science methodological approaches was used to collect and analyze data in this study. This strengthens the work considerably by providing triangulation on the phenomena observed and measured.

The Study Population

The California Office of Emergency Services identified all or portions of seven counties as "areas at risk" in the event that the Parkfield earthquake was a magnitude 7.0: Monterey, San Benito, western Fresno, Kings, San Luis Obispo, western Kern, and Santa Barbara counties. More than a dozen cities and towns and some 122,000 households fell within this risk area. Communities in these counties were different distances from the predicted epicenter of the Parkfield earthquake, and they had different historical experiences with damaging earthquakes. Consequently, distance and experience served as stratification factors in the selection of study communities.

The Samples

The following sections describe how specific study communities were selected, the sampling frames for community households, how the actual household samples were selected, and how the representativeness of each sample was assessed.

Selection of Study Communities

Prior research has clearly confirmed that distance from risk is influential in altering both public perception and response to risk communications (Danzig, Thayer, and Galater 1958; Mileti, Hutton, and Sorensen 1981; Zeigler and Johnson 1984). Researchers have also long suspected that disaster experience influences both risk perception and response to subsequent communications about risk (Fogleman 1958; Perry and Greene 1982). Therefore, communities selected for study had to fall within the identified area of risk, had to be somewhat similar in size, and had to vary by distance from the epicenter of the predicted earthquake and by prior experience with a damaging earthquake.

Parkfield itself was not considered for inclusion as a study community even though it is closest to the predicted quake's epicenter because Parkfield is a small community of three-dozen people, most of whom are children, and because research on these citizens' responses to the prediction had already been completed (Mileti and Hutton 1986).

Coalinga and Paso Robles are the towns of any appreciable size closest to the predicted epicenter. They are both about 25 miles from Parkfield. Coalinga had a devastating earthquake in 1983, and its inclusion as a study community provided an opportunity to represent in the study a community with recent experience with a damaging earthquake. Inclusion of Paso Robles provided a comparison group for Coalinga because it is equally distant from the predicted epicenter but without recent earthquake disaster experience. Inclusion of these two communities permitted us to compare risk perception and response to the prediction across communities at like distances to the predicted epicenter, but with and without recent earthquake disaster experience.

A third town, Taft, is located approximately 75 miles from the predicted epicenter yet still falls within the identified area at risk. Taft is about the same size as Coalinga and Paso Robles yet has no recent earthquake disaster experience. Taft was included as a study community to provide a comparison to a community without close proximity or earthquake experience.

Results from the three selected communities permitted comparisons of distance from the risk (Paso Robles versus Taft) and of recent damaging earthquake experience (Coalinga versus Paso Robles). Results also permitted comparisons of the combination of experience and distance when Coalinga was compared to Taft. This approach is a preexperimental field research design (Campbell and Stanley 1963). Its use permitted us to control for some relevant variables through the sampling procedure rather than through the use of statistical tests. Controlling for variables in this way strengthens the conclusions that can be drawn regarding the causal effect of experience and distance. Although this research design is one of the strongest, an opportunity to use this sort of design is infrequent in social science research.

Household Sampling Frames and Samples

The California Office of Emergency Services (OES) contracted with a private firm to send out the Parkfield prediction brochure to all 122,000 residential addresses in the seven-county area at-risk. We purchased an identical copy of the mailing list used by that firm to select household samples for study. We extracted a complete enumeration of all residential addresses for each of the three study communities by using the zip codes of our selected study communities.

The household samples for each community were drawn in a systematically random manner from each of those community sampling frames. The first household for inclusion in the sample for each community was randomly selected. Successive addresses were then drawn on the basis of a sampling fraction specific to each community. The sampling fraction was constructed so that the resulting approximate sample would be 1,200 households in each study community. We anticipated that a sample of 1,200 households in each study community would yield at least 400 returned questionnaires from each community. We judged that 400 returned questionnaires would constitute an adequate number to statistically represent all of the households in each study community (Blalock and Blalock 1968). These procedures yielded sampling fractions of one in three for Coalinga and one in six for Paso Robles and Taft. The actual number of households selected for sample inclusion was 1,149 for Coalinga, 1,106 for Paso Robles, and 1,056 for Taft.

The actual size of the samples was reduced for reasons that did not affect the samples' representativeness. For example, addresses were lost from the sampling frame due to nondelivered mail because of incorrect addresses or vacant residences, addresses that were not households but were churches or businesses; and we made a decision to exclude post office boxes to prevent double sampling of households. The final sample sizes, after addresses were excluded for the above-listed reasons, were as follows: 662 for Coalinga, 887 for Paso Robles, and 756 for Taft. A total of 347 questionnaires were returned from Coalinga, 357 were returned from Paso Robles, and 234 were returned from Taft. These figures represent response rates of 52.4%, 40.2%, and 31.0%, respectively. These response rates are somewhat lower than what would ordinarily be expected from the mailing procedures we used for data collection.

Assessment of Representativeness

We attempted a comparison of the samples' demographic characteristics with 1980 census data on gender, tenancy, age, ethnicity, household size, and household income. However, data limitations prevented a complete analysis. The census data were nearly 10 years old, which meant comparing the demographic profile of the communities in 1989 with what it had been in 1980. Some census data were available only at the county level and not for the city. These could not be compared because to do so would have meant comparing demographic profiles of an entire county with city characteristics. We had no reason to believe the county and city data were comparable. The following conclusions were made on the basis of the comparisons that we were able to perform.

Regarding gender, we found that our Coalinga sample over represented females by about 9%, our Paso Robles sample under represented females by about 4%, and our Taft sample over represented females by about 11%. With respect to age, we found that our Coalinga sample over represented senior citizens (age 65 and older) by about 11%, our Paso Robles sample over represented them by about 19%, and our Taft sample by about 8%. With reference to ethnicity, our Coalinga sample under represented nonwhites by about 4%, our Paso Robles sample under represented nonwhites by about 3%, and our Taft sample represented whites and nonwhites, almost exactly matching their census distribution.

For all three communities, the household size of the samples matched the census data almost perfectly. The average number of persons per household, according to the 1980 census, for Coalinga was 2.76, whereas it was 2.70 in our Coalinga sample. The census average number of persons per household for Paso Robles was 2.51, whereas it was 2.46 in our Paso Robles sample. And the census average number of persons per household for Taft was 2.48, whereas it was 2.56 in our Taft sample. We concluded from this that the community samples did not markedly over represent senior citizens; if they had, the household-size characteristics of the samples would differ more from the census data than was the case. The differences observed between age structure from 1980 to 1989 may simply have been due to an aging population.

The observed differences between the demographic characteristics of the community samples and the 1980 census data appeared to us to be like those that are characteristic of most mail questionnaire surveys. The community samples were not perfectly representative of the demographic profiles of the study communities. Additionally, our questionnaires were distributed in English. This would have excluded from participation persons not able to read English and nonliterate persons.

Bias in our samples was not profound, but it was there. Sampling bias is a particular problem in research such as ours if it results in minimizing variation on a variable in a tested hypothesis. For example, there would be a problem if bias excluded poor people from a sample if income was used in a hypothesis to predict a dependent variable such as risk perception. If poor people are less likely to perceive risk than middle-class or very affluent people, the exclusion of the poor from a data set would lead to the incorrect conclusion that income has no effect on risk perception when that hypothesis is tested. Consequently, we took care to ensure sufficient variation on all variables used to test hypotheses so that no hypothesis would be accepted or rejected because of sample bias.

Data Collection

Qualitative and quantitative data collection methods were used in this research. The following sections review the techniques used to collect both types of data.

Descriptive Fieldwork

Field investigations were conducted in each study community in January 1989 to profile the full range of risk information available to the public about both the Parkfield earthquake prediction and earthquakes in general. Our fieldwork used a variety of techniques to collect qualitative data on relevant public information. Unobtrusive measures such as written materials and records were used as much as possible (Webb *et al.* 1966). We obtained relevant newspaper clippings from the Southern California Earthquake Preparedness Project in Los Angeles. Community artifacts were also collected, including earthquake response plans, brochures, comic books, and other materials available to the public at county offices of emergency services and local offices of the American Red Cross. We collected and reviewed available scripts and tapes of relevant radio and television broadcasts. We interviewed knowledgeable local officials and media staff regarding publicly available information about the earthquake prediction and about earthquake readiness. Additional interviews were conducted with staffs in city government, fire departments, county offices of emergency services, schools and school district offices, American Red Cross offices, and radio and television stations. Approximately 36 interviews of this type were performed.

Obtaining information from the broadcast media proved to be more difficult than anticipated. Although Federal Communications Commission (FCC) regulations require that public service announcements be logged, considerable clerical time would have been needed to review the logs for all the relevant information. Furthermore, radio and television stations did not necessarily maintain tape libraries of their entire programming. Given these constraints, we approximated local television and radio coverage in the study communities by working with cooperative broadcasters.

This descriptive fieldwork enabled us to catalog a rich array of the kinds of information made public regarding the Parkfield earthquake prediction in our study communities. This information was used in formulating the questions asked on our household questionnaire.

The Questionnaire

The questionnaire was constructed to collect quantitative household-level data on the concepts included in each of the study's hypotheses. The Dillman (1978) method guided questionnaire construction to enhance response rates. We attended to both the content and form of the questionnaire to make it as attractive as possible. Within a printed booklet, we employed simplicity, a smooth flow of questions, clear instruction, and transitional phrases to make the data collection instrument understandable. We used clear printing and numbering sequences to create an orderly impression. Response categories were exhaustive and mutually exclusive. In a word, we designed the mail questionnaire to be as user friendly as possible.

The questionnaire was pretested through review by Parkfield residents and by policymakers in California communities, and was subsequently revised in keeping with reviewer comments. Each community's questionnaire booklet was printed with a different-colored cover to make returned questionnaires easy to code by community. Included with each questionnaire was a cover letter and a stamped self-addressed envelope for respondent convenience in returning completed questionnaires.

Sample households first received a postcard alerting them that they had been selected to be part of a scientific study on public response to the earthquake prediction. The postcards were mailed April 10-12, 1989. The first mailing of questionnaires took place April 24-28, 1989. Follow-up postcards were mailed May 13-20, 1989. The second and final follow-up questionnaires were mailed June 14-19, 1989.

Data were cleaned and coded using a computer program written especially for this data set. The community data sets were input twice by two independent coders; the resulting two data sets were scrutinized by computer for differences, and the differences were resolved. The cleaned data were stored for analysis using the Statistical Package for the Social Sciences (SPSS/PC+) program.

Data Analysis

The quantitative data from household questionnaires were analyzed in four ways: (1) descriptive analysis showed proportions of respondents having done or thought the things we asked about, (2) comparative analysis statistically compared grouped community responses to determine if the factors of experience and distance affected what people thought and did in response to the prediction, (3) multiple regression analysis tested the individual risk communication hypotheses suggested by the literature, and (4) path analysis determined the major causal paths that linked getting information about the prediction through a variety of intervening factors to explain and predict actual public response to the prediction.

Descriptive Analysis

The descriptive analysis was straightforward. We selected measures of all variables we sought to describe that were measured on an interval scale. This enabled the descriptive data to be presented as percentages for each study community. Observed response patterns within and across communities were then identified and discussed.

Comparative Analysis

The comparative analysis used the Student's *t*-tests for analyzing the difference-of-means on selected variables between the study communities. This statistical test was selected for several reasons.

First, each study community had a different number of respondents and *t*-tests do not require an equal number of respondents in each group being compared to assess for statistical differences (Klockars and Sax 1986). Second, the true population parameters from which the samples were drawn were not known. Consequently, the *t*-distribution would yield more confidence than the normal curve in drawing conclusions about the data being examined (Leonard 1976). Third, the variances in each population from which the samples were drawn could not be assumed to be equal; the *t*-test is one of the most appropriate statistics for testing difference-of-means between groups under this circumstance. A separate-variance *t*-test was used to test all hypothesized difference-of-means between the independent samples because we could not confidently assume equal variance between compared groups on all variables being compared. A one-tailed test was used because each hypothesis being tested had direction.

The Student's *t*-test provides information on significant differences between means, but it does not yield information on the strength of the relationship. The strength of a relationship can be inferred from how close the observations in each group are to the mean of that group. In measuring the strength of the relationship, we sought to improve the prediction of a dependent variable by knowing the group to which respondents belonged. Improvement in predictions comes from determining the difference between the loss derived from the total sum of squares (TSS) when the group to which households belong is unknown and the loss derived from the residual sum of squares (RSS) when the group to which households belong is known. This improvement in prediction is called *eta*. The square route of *eta* (eta^2) becomes a measure of the strength of a relationship. Both *eta* and eta^2 are interpreted the same as r and r^2 in regression analysis (Iversen 1979).

These statistical techniques were used to determine the presence of statistically significant differences between communities. Differences were assessed on factors of perception and behavior in response to the prediction. Patterns of significant community differences were observed. These patterns were then interpreted in terms of how the factors of disaster experience and distance to the predicted quake's epicenter affected what people thought and did after being informed about the anticipated earthquake. The effect of experience was assessed on the basis of Coalinga-Paso Robles comparisons. The impact of distance was determined by comparing responses in Paso Robles to those in Taft. The interactive effect of experience and distance was inferred from Coalinga-Taft comparisons.

Multiple Regression Analysis

The ordinary least squares (OLS) estimating technique was used in all multiple regression tests performed. This technique is based on several assumptions.

First, OLS assumes that there is no specification error in an equation, which suggests that the relationships between variables are linear, no relevant independent variables have been excluded from the equation, and no irrelevant independent variables have been included in the equation. OLS also assumes that there is no measurement error; that the error term for the dependent variable has a mean of zero; and that it is homoscedastic, without auto correlation, not correlated with the independent variables, and normally distributed (Lewis-Beck 1980). Regression coefficient estimates are best linear unbiased estimates (BLUE) when these assumptions can be met.

Multiple regression analysis in this study had a straightforward application: It was used to determine the predictive value of alternative types of one set of independent variable categories against separate dependent variables taken one at a time. For example, one multiple regression equation was run to determine which channels of prediction information (television, radio, newspapers, the brochure, face-to-face communication, and so on) affected a dependent variable (for example, belief in the prediction). This use of multiple regression enabled us to determine the major factors that shaped public perception and response to the Parkfield earthquake prediction; it also allowed us to compare findings across each of the three communities and determine quickly which of the many risk communication hypotheses being tested could be accepted or rejected.

We dismissed as not important any independent variables that were consistently, across all three study communities, not significantly related to any of the dependent variables examined. We also dismissed independent variables that resulted in marginal and inconsistent effects on a dependent variable. For example, an independent variable was seen as marginal if it did not have a significant effect on a dependent variable across all communities, if its effect on a dependent variable was very weak in the community where it did display a significant relationship to a dependent variable, and where we could conclude that it played a very minor statistical and theoretically insignificant role in explaining the dependent variable or variables under examination. Comparable findings across communities and some unique findings within communities were thus identified and explained.

This application of the multiple regression technique did not markedly differ from the computation of zero-order correlation coefficients between independent and dependent variables. Estimated regression coefficients for each independent variable in a multiple regression equation are identical to zero-order correlation coefficients. Multiple regression equations were calculated instead of individual zero-order correlations because they provided a handy way to group categories of independent variables. This made data analysis easier. The strength and statistical significance of individual multiple regression coefficients were interpreted. Although the explained variance for each equation is reported, this estimated parameter of the equations must be interpreted carefully. Explained variance in a multiple regression equation can be artificially deflated due to the direction of the relationships between individual independent variables in an equation on the dependent variable. This effect does not affect the strength or statistical significance of individual coefficients within each equation.

Path Analysis

Path analysis attempts to use a series of interlocking multiple regression equations in order to resolve questions "about possible causes by providing explanations of phenomena (effects) as the result of previous phenomena (causes)" (Asher 1983, p. 5). No statistical technique can extract causal proof from a data set; however, path analysis can model a set of inter-related theoretical propositions, simultaneously estimate the equations representing the theory, and provide answers regarding the relative magnitude of linkages in the model, suggesting insights into what may be underlying causal processes. Multiple correlation coefficients indicate how much of a particular dependent variable in the model has been explained by the set of independent variables and alternative causal paths to that dependent variable contained in the model.

Path analysis was used to model the basic risk communication theory that informed this research and to determine which variables and paths of causal influence provided the greatest ability to explain and predict what the public thought and did in response to the Parkfield earthquake prediction.

Appendix C

A Causal Explanation of Response

Causality is difficult to establish in the social sciences, even when statistical analyses are done on data that are part of the experimental method. Causal modeling based on cross-sectional data such as those used in this research can reveal the most significant statistical paths influencing action and can implement relatively complex sets of statistical controls. These controls enable determination of the effect of relationships between variables contained in a model to be determined while holding constant all other variables in the model.

The causal modeling performed in this investigation draws together all the factors suggested by risk communication theory, focuses only on those factors suggested as important in the multiple regression analysis, and clarifies the processes that best explain public prediction response. This was accomplished by using path analytic techniques, that is, simultaneous multiple regression equations.

The General Prediction Response Model

The general model constructed to guide the path analysis is presented in Figure C.1. This model subsumes the factors and the relationships among them suggested by theory and past research and the reconceptualizations in theory suggested by our regression analyses (see Appendix B). The model proposes that public mitigation and preparedness behavior in response to the prediction was a direct consequence of (1) the kind of information people received about the risk and what to do, (2) their own personal characteristics, (3) the perceptions people held, and (4) their information-seeking behavior about the risk and what to do. Information-seeking was cast as a consequence of information received, personal characteristics of those receiving the information, and perceptions. Finally, risk perceptions were modeled as a result of received information and personal characteristics.

Figure C.1 The General Path Model for Public Prediction Response[*]

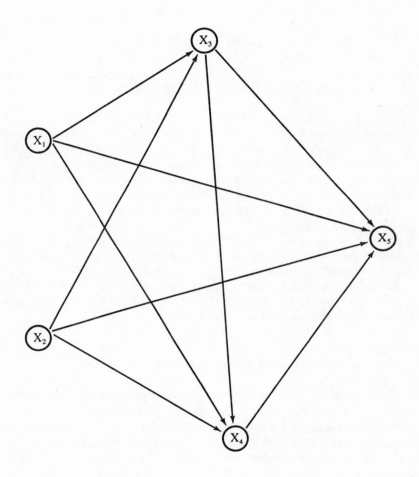

[*]Where X_1 = information or "sender" factors about what was communicated to the public, X_2 = "receiver" factors about the characteristics of the people who received the communications, X_3 = the perceptions people held, X_4 = the information-seeking behavior in which people engaged, and X_5 = the mitigation and preparedness behavior that people actually performed.

Unfortunately, the concept of "hearing" about the prediction had to be excluded from our sample data—most people had heard about the Parkfield prediction. The personal characteristic of community integration was also excluded from the model, since it only had an effect on hearing about the prediction and not on the other risk communication process factors included.

This model is parsimonious, since it contains five theoretical constructs that represent dozens of factors known to be important to the process of risk communication and public response. The model also subsumes all factors that our prior analyses suggested were consistently relevant in our data sets. Although the model is simple enough to understand and interpret, it is far from being operationalized into a form that could be statistically estimated.

Operationalizing the Model

The general model presented in Figure C.1 lacks sufficient specification to enable it to be subjected to empirical test. For example, it is composed of general constructs (like information factors) that stand for far more than one variable. These constructs actually represent many specific variables (e.g., information factors represent variables like information specificity, understandability, and the number of communications received). This model must be brought down the ladder of abstraction to enable it to include the fuller array of relevant factors suggested by theory and prior research, and to be statistically estimated.

When we considered the full array of variables of significance in operationalizing the general theoretical model, we saw a model which could be tested empirically, but it was so complex as to be uninterpretable. Additionally, this model contained so many variables that it violated practical statistical assumptions that must be met in order to trust the information produced by such an analysis. For example, explained variance in any endogenous variable in the model would be influenced by having exogenous variables in any one equation; it would be hard to know if explained variance was attributable to the discovery of significant causal paths of influence between variables or simply to having included too many exogenous variables in any one equation.

The dilemma was straightforward: The more factors included in the operationalized empirical model, the more that model would represent what we believe influences behavior in the real world; however, the more factors included, the less intelligible and statistically accurate would be our findings.

Obviously, the operationalization of the general model had to tap the rich set of factors subsumed by the model's general concepts. At the same time, the operationalized model had to maintain statistical integrity and understandability and be parsimonious. An operationalized model was needed that was practical, theoretically complete, and correctly specified. Two strategies were used to achieve such a model.

The first was to operationalize the model at the mid-range. For example, instead of proposing a model that included all relevant variables as unique factors, we operationalized the model at a higher level of abstraction with concepts that subsumed relevant individual variables. This approach produced a theoretically correct model, maintained parsimony, and still provided a vehicle whereby a statistically correct model could be produced. At the same time, this strategy enabled inclusion in the model of any and all collected data on variables subsumed by the mid-range concepts.

The second strategy was grounded in the empirical fit of the data with existing theory. It was possible to reduce greatly the number of variables in the operationalized model by excluding those that had no consistent statistical effect on any of the factors under consideration. For example, the multiple regression analyses illustrated that variables like occupational prestige and level of education did not relate to the dependent variables of risk perception, information-seeking, or mitigation and preparedness behaviors. Therefore, there was no reason to include these variables in the operationalized model, since they did not fit the data gathered in this study.

The Operationalized Model

The operationalized model used to direct the path analysis of prediction response is presented in Figure C.2. This model includes the two major personal, or receiver, characteristics that best fit these data: preprediction earthquake hazard salience, and postprediction contextual cues. Two information, or sender, characteristics are also in the model: the frequency and divergence in the prediction messages received and message style. The model casts mitigation and preparedness response (X_7) as a function of information-seeking, risk perception, message style, message frequency, contextual cues, and preprediction salience. Information-seeking (X_6) is the consequence of risk perception, message style, message frequency, contextual cues, and preprediction salience. Risk perception is the result of message style, message frequency, contextual cues, and preprediction salience.

Figure C.2 The Operationalized Path Model for Public Prediction Response*

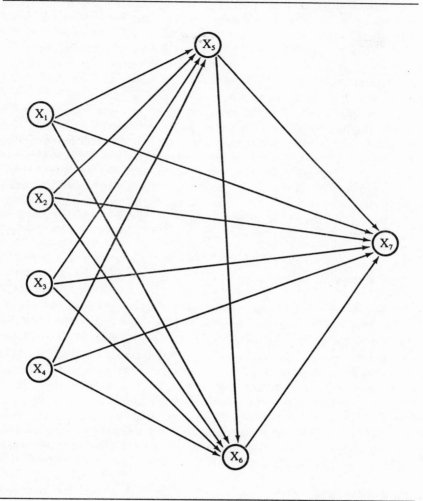

*Where X_1 = preprediction salience, X_2 = contextual cues, X_3 = frequency of receipt of prediction messages, X_4 = message style, X_5 = perception of risk, X_6 = information-seeking, and X_7 = mitigation- and preparedness-readiness behavior.

The operationalized model excludes other factors that were shown in the multiple regression analysis to not affect prediction response, directly or indirectly. It composes mid-range concepts that subsume several other less abstract variables. This required that scales be constructed from the study's measures to represent the concepts contained in the model.

The construction of scales involved the addition of scores across two or more measures. Obviously, many of the factors added to construct a composite scale were not additive in the sense of basic arithmetic. For example, adding an information-content score to an information-source score presumes equality in these two information attributes, and equality may not exist. All added scores used original scales that had a zero starting point. The use of the resulting composite scales enabled the inclusion of multiple indicators for a concept and the reduction of the number of factors in the model, and it dramatically enhanced the parsimony of the operationalized model. We judged that the merits of this approach far outweighed any shortcomings. The following sections describe how each concept in the operationalized model was measured and scaled.

Preprediction Salience

Preprediction salience was measured by asking respondents about a range of mitigation and preparedness actions that they could have taken because of the earthquake hazard but before the issuance of the Parkfield prediction. Asked about were purchasing earthquake insurance, anchoring the house to its foundation, stockpiling emergency supplies, developing an emergency family plan, and eight other mitigation and preparedness actions. These actions were intervally coded and varied between 0 (no preprediction actions taken) and 12 (all types of actions asked about were taken). We thought that the salience of the earthquake hazard was indicated by the actions a respondent had taken to mitigate the hazards and prepare for future earthquakes.

Contextual Cues

Contextual cues were measured dichotomously by using respondents' answers to the following question: "Do you know of anyone (for example, friends, relatives, or neighbors) who has done anything to get ready for the Parkfield earthquake (for example, made their home or possessions safer)?"

Frequency of Receipt of Prediction Messages

Persons who participated in the study were asked to tell us the channels of communication through which they received information about the earthquake prediction, as well as from whom they received information. Communication channels included television, radio, newspapers, magazines, brochures, posters, meetings, and informal conversations. Information sources included informal sources (friends, relatives, neighbors), government sources (city, county, state, federal), scientists, the Red Cross, and other sources (fire departments, schools, utility companies).

A frequency scale was constructed by adding the number of different channels through which people had gotten prediction information to the number of different sources from which information had been received. This index, therefore, combined the important channel and source dimensions of risk communication; its use allowed us to include a great deal of information in the model.

Message Style

We also sought to develop a composite scale for the varied style attributes associated with communicated risk information. Two style attributes were revealed as important by the multiple regression analyses: message specificity and consistency. Message specificity was measured by asking respondents about information contained in the official prediction brochure mailed to households regarding damage estimates, probability, time window, ability to feel the earthquake, what people had been advised to do to mitigate and prepare, and several specific aspects about the short-term warning that might be issued. A total of 39 individual items on the questionnaire covered these information attributes. These were summed for each respondent based on the logic that the more of these items a respondent reported hearing, the more specific was the risk information which the respondent perceived or remembered. This score was given weight equal to the dichotomous measure of risk information consistency. Consistency was measured by asking respondents if they agreed with the following statement: "Earthquake scientists agree about the Parkfield earthquake prediction." The index of message style, therefore, was equally indicative of both consistency and specificity of risk information.

Risk Perception. The risk that people perceive regarding a future earthquake is a complex concept. Prior research and theory revealed that two important elements of risk perception are belief in the prediction and personalization of risk. An index of risk perception was constructed that included both of these elements. Belief was measured by asking the question, "Do you believe that scientists can predict earthquakes?" Risk personalization was measured by asking respondents if they thought there would be an earthquake that caused them economic losses and/or physical harm in their lifetimes and/or in the next few years. Responses were coded in terms of personalized Parkfield earthquake risk, which ranged from "I will not experience an earthquake in my lifetime that causes me or someone in my family economic losses" (the lowest risk personalization category) to "I will experience an earthquake in the next few years that causes me or someone in my family physical harm" (the highest risk personalization category). Belief and personalization scores were then added to create an index of risk perception that included both perceptual elements.

Information-Seeking. The scale constructed for seeking more information was based on public attempts to obtain more information about both earthquake prediction and what to do to get ready for earthquakes. Respondents reported attempts to get more information about the science of earthquake prediction and about preparing for the quake from government agencies, from nongovernment agencies, and from informal groups and associates like friends and relatives. These data were used to construct a 17-point scale ranging from zero for no information-seeking to six for seeking information about both topics from all three sources.

Mitigation and Preparedness Response. Respondents were asked about six mitigation and six preparedness actions they could have taken after the Parkfield prediction was issued. Each of these actions was recommended in the public prediction brochure, for example, purchase earthquake insurance and stockpile emergency supplies. These dozen factors were added to create a mitigation and preparedness readiness score that ranged from zero (no recommended actions taken) to 12 (all recommended actions taken).

Assessment of Data Quality

The measures used to construct scales and the scales themselves were assessed to determine data quality. Data used in path analyses yield more accurate and trustworthy results when they have certain characteristics. For example, each measure and scale should possess variation across the range, be able to be treated as if it were an interval scale, and not have an oversized standard error. The data used in this analysis conformed to these requisites. Additionally, path analysis also requires that reasonable assumptions can be met regarding issues like the lack of strong multi-colinearity among exogenous variables, the lack of specification error, and the presence of homoscedasticity (see Lewis-Beck 1980). The data used in the path analysis were assessed for their ability to conform to these assumptions and were judged to be adequate for the ordinary least squares (OLS) estimation technique.

Data and Findings

The operationalized model (see Figure C.2) was represented by the following equations:

$$X_5 = \beta_{51}X_1 + \beta_{52}X_2 + \beta_{53}X_3 + \beta_{54}X_4 + e_5$$
$$X_6 = \beta_{61}X_1 + \beta_{62}X_2 + \beta_{63}X_3 + \beta_{64}X_4 + \beta_{65}X_5 + e_6$$
$$X_7 = \beta_{71}X_1 + \beta_{72}X_2 + \beta_{73}X_3 + \beta_{74}X_4 + \beta_{75}X_5 + \beta_{76}X_6 + e_7$$

The model was estimated for each study community. The estimated model parameters include path coefficients (betas), explained variance for each equation, and other estimates; these are presented in Table C.1, Table C.2, and Table C.3, respectively, for Taft, Paso Robles, and Coalinga. The data sets for all three study communities were not combined, since each sample had different variances. If the data sets were to be combined, the resulting data could not represent any group or population, since path estimates are affected by alternative variances across samples. Consequently, the path estimates across the three study communities cannot be compared; however, the theoretical conclusion from each study community can be compared.

The estimated parameters of the models for Taft, Paso Robles, and Coalinga reveal the relative success of the model in explaining public perception and response in all three study communities. The explained variance for risk perception was 18%, 8%, and 7%, respectively, for Taft, Paso Robles, and Coalinga; the explained variance in information-seeking was 39%, 25%, and 20%, and was 35%, 28%, and 29% for mitigation and preparedness readiness response to the prediction. These are relatively high explained variances for a study based on data gathered from individuals, and they confirm the predictive power of the model.

An amazingly consistent set of conclusions can be drawn from these data. These conclusions confirm many parts of established risk communication theory and add new insights to knowledge about communicating risk information to the public. The general conclusions are presented in diagram form in Figure C.3.

Table C.1 Estimated Parameters of the Model for Taft[*]

Endogenous Variables	Exogenous Variables	r	Path Coeff.	Est.	α	R^2
X_5	X_1	.29	β_{51}	.19	.00	.18
	X_2	.29	β_{52}	.18		
	X_3	.33	β_{53}	.15		
	X_4	.30	β_{54}	.18		
X_6	X_1	.28	β_{61}	n/s	.00	.39
	X_2	.39	β_{62}	.20		
	X_3	.52	β_{63}	.39		
	X_4	.35	β_{64}	n/s		
	X_5	.44	β_{65}	.24		
X_7	X_1	.11	β_{71}	n/s	.00	.35
	X_2	.33	β_{72}	.13		
	X_3	.30	β_{73}	n/s		
	X_4	.28	β_{74}	.13		
	X_5	.30	β_{75}	n/s		
	X_6	.60	β_{76}	.54		

[*]Where X_1 = preprediction salience, X_2 = contextual cues, X_3 = frequency of receipt of prediction messages, X_4 = message style, X_5 = perception of risk, X_6 = information-seeking, and X_7 = mitigation- and preparedness-readiness behavior.

Table C.2   Estimated Parameters of the Model for Paso Robles[*]

Endogenous Variables	Exogenous Variables	r	Path Coeff.	Est.	α	R^2
X_5	X_1	.20	β_{51}	.17	.00	.08
	X_2	.08	β_{52}	n/s		
	X_3	.13	β_{53}	n/s		
	X_4	.25	β_{54}	.23		
X_6	X_1	.18	β_{61}	n/s	.00	.25
	X_2	.27	β_{62}	.19		
	X_3	.44	β_{63}	.40		
	X_4	.22	β_{64}	n/s		
	X_5	.25	β_{65}	.16		
X_7	X_1	.12	β_{71}	n/s	.00	.28
	X_2	.25	β_{72}	.11		
	X_3	.26	β_{73}	n/s		
	X_4	.24	β_{74}	.10		
	X_5	.25	β_{75}	.02		
	X_6	.50	β_{76}	.48		

[*]Where X_1 = preprediction salience, X_2 = contextual cues, X_3 = frequency of receipt of prediction messages, X_4 = message style, X_5 = perception of risk, X_6 = information-seeking, and X_7 = mitigation- and preparedness-readiness behavior.

Table C.3　Estimated Parameters of the Model for Coalinga[*]

Endogenous Variables	Exogenous Variables	r	Path Coeff.	Est.	α	R^2
X_5	X_1	.21	β_{51}	.12	.00	.07
	X_2	.21	β_{52}	.12		
	X_3	.23	β_{53}	.13		
	X_4	.14	β_{54}	n/s		
X_6	X_1	.15	β_{61}	n/s	.00	.20
	X_2	.28	β_{62}	.16		
	X_3	.36	β_{63}	.25		
	X_4	.21	β_{64}	n/s		
	X_5	.31	β_{65}	.22		
X_7	X_1	-.06	β_{71}	-.17	.00	.29
	X_2	.22	β_{72}	.14		
	X_3	.15	β_{73}	n/s		
	X_4	.04	β_{74}	n/s		
	X_5	.16	β_{75}	n/s		
	X_6	.51	β_{76}	.51		

[*]Where X_1 = preprediction salience, X_2 = contextual cues, X_3 = frequency of receipt of prediction messages, X_4 = message style, X_5 = perception of risk, X_6 = information-seeking, and X_7 = mitigation- and preparedness-readiness behavior.

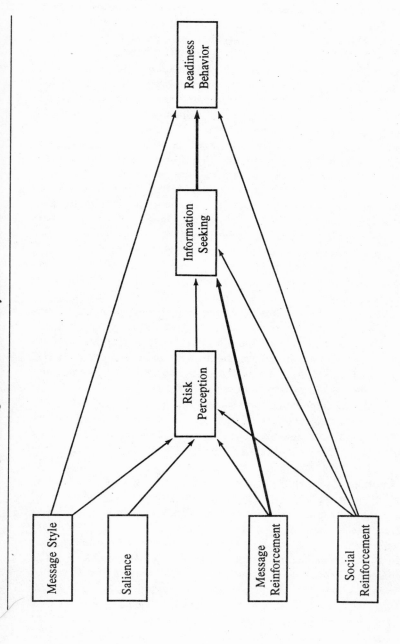

Figure C.3 Common Findings Resulting from the Path Analyses*

*Where thicker lines represent major causal paths in the estimated parameters of the models for all three study communities.

Validity is lent to general risk communication theory when the relationships in the models are examined. In general, risk communication theory suggests that (1) risk perception in response to communicated information is the result of both sender and receiver factors, (2) information-seeking or confirmation is the result of sender and receiver factors as well as perceived risk, and (3) actual public response to communicated information is a consequence of sender and receiver factors, as well as perceived risk and information-seeking or confirmation. In general, each of these sets of relationships existed in the model estimates for all three study communities.

Risk perception was the consequence of both sender and receiver factors, as suggested by risk communication theory. For example, risk perception (belief and personalization) was the result of salience in all three communities: β_{51} for Taft, Paso Robles, and Coalinga was .19, .17 and .12, respectively. Message style (consistency and specificity) also affected risk perception in Taft ($\beta_{54} = .18$) and Paso Robles ($\beta_{54} = .23$), but not in Coalinga. Message style is an important factor in risk communication; however, it seems that in places like Coalinga, where salience is high due to experience, risk perception (belief and personalization) results from any message style that is heard. Finally, risk perception was the result of message reinforcement and frequency ($\beta_{53} = .15$ for Taft and .13 for Coalinga) and contextual reinforcement or cues ($\beta_{52} = .18$ for Taft and .12 for Coalinga) in Taft and Coalinga, but not in Paso Robles. Reinforcement did not affect risk perception in Paso Robles, perhaps since people in Paso Robles were more prone to deny risk because of their close proximity to the predicted quake's epicenter and because they lacked recent experience.

Receiver factors (contextual cues or reinforcement and salience of the earthquake hazard before the prediction was issued) and sender factors (message style and message frequency or reinforcement) both enhanced the perceptions people held about risk (belief and personalization). This is exactly what risk communication theory would predict. Exceptions seem to be that people with recent experience are likely to perceive risk regardless of message style because of their experience; reinforcement of the risk message does not overcome the tendency of people to deny risk if they are close to the risk's potential impact.

Information-seeking, as would be predicted from existing theory, was the result of receiver factors, sender factors, and risk perception. The receiver factor of contextual cues or reinforcement was positively related to information-seeking in all three study communities (β_{62} was .20 for Taft, .19 for Paso Robles, and .16 for Coalinga). The same was the case for message reinforcement, where β_{63} was .39 for Taft, .40 for Paso Robles, and .25 for Coalinga. Finally, risk perception enhanced information-seeking in all three communities (β_{65} was .24 in Taft, .16 in Paso Robles, and .22 in Coalinga).

Performance of mitigation and preparedness tasks (risk-reduction actions) was the direct consequence of information-seeking (β_{76} was .54 for Taft, .48 for Paso Robles, and .51 for Coalinga) and contextual cues or reinforcement (β_{72} was .13 for Taft, .11 for Paso Robles, and .14 for Coalinga). Additionally, message style had a positive effect on response in both communities without recent earthquake experience (β_{74} was .13 in Taft and .10 in Paso Robles), but not in Coalinga. Message style had no impact in Coalinga probably because the hazard was salient for people due to experience. Salience had a negative impact on response ($\beta_{71} = -.17$) only in Coalinga because salience was measured by preprediction readiness activities, which Coalinga residents had already engaged in after the earthquake in the mid-1980s. People who mitigated and prepared following the earthquake but before the prediction did not have to do so after the prediction.

Conclusions

The most interesting results are the causal paths discovered in the models and not the effects of individual factors on separate dependent communities. The strongest causal paths in the models for all three study communities were identical. In each study community, mitigation and preparedness actions were primarily a consequence of people engaging in information-seeking on their own. The beta coefficients (β_{76}) for this relationship for Taft, Paso Robles, and Coalinga, respectively, were .54, .48, and .51. Additionally, again consistently across all three communities, information-seeking was itself more a consequence of information reinforcement than of anything else. Message frequency in the models was operationalized as the reinforcement of communicated information by the receipt of multiple messages through diverse channels and from varied sources. The beta coefficients (β_{63}) for this relationship for Taft, Paso Robles, and Coalinga, respectively, were .39, .40, and .25. An alternative form of reinforcement of Communicated information was also reinforced by cues. This factor was operationalized as knowing others who were actually mitigating and preparing for the earthquake. The beta coefficients (β_{62}) for this relationship for Taft, Paso Robles, and Coalinga, respectively, were .20, .19, and .16.

Risk communication about the Parkfield earthquake prediction was most effective when it was a process of multiple messages delivered through multiple channels and emanating from multiple sources. This communication process reinforced the risk and the need to consider mitigation and preparedness actions. Reinforcement of the risk was accomplished through multiple and diverse communications. Reinforcement of the risk and the need to consider actions also resulted from contextual cues, or knowing the people who were acting to mitigate and prepare.

Reinforced, communicated information was indirectly a cause of protective action through its effect on a significant intervening factor: seeking additional information on one's own. The act of searching for additional information about the risk, the prediction, and what to do produced personal ideas and definitions about what to do. The key causal findings from all three Parkfield earthquake prediction study communities are the same: (1) communicated public risk information that was reinforced precipitated an interactive public search for more information, (2) personal definitions about what to do emerged from this search, and (3) the resulting personal definitions and ideas about what to do directed what people actually did in response to the earthquake prediction.

References

Ad Hoc Interagency Working Group for Earthquake Research. 1967. *Proposal for a Ten-Year National Earthquake Hazard Program.* Washington, DC: Federal Council for Science and Technology.

Ad Hoc Panel on Earthquake Prediction. 1965. *Earthquake Prediction: A Proposal for a Ten Year Program of Research.* Washington, DC: Office of Science and Technology.

Allen, Clarence. 1982. "Earthquake Prediction — 1982 Overview." *Bulletin of Seismological Society of America* 72(December):S331-S335.

Anderson, William A., and Charles C. Thiel. 1979. "The Response of Social Institutions to Earthquake Prediction." Paper presented at the International Symposium on Earthquake Prediction. Paris, France: UNESCO Headquarters (26 February).

Asher, Herbert B. 1983. *Causal Modelling.* SAGE Publications Series on Quantitative Applications in the Social Sciences. Beverly Hills, CA: Sage Publications.

Atwood, L. Erwin. 1991. "The Great Media Earthquake of 1990: Third-Person Effects." Paper presented at the Conference on Public and Media Response to Earthquake Forecasts, Southern Illinois University at Edwardsville, May 16-18. Carbondale, IL: Southern Illinois University at Carbondale, School of Journalism.

Ayre, Robert S., Dennis S. Mileti, and Patricia B. Trainer. 1975. *Earthquake and Tsunami Hazards in the United States: A Research Assessment.* Boulder, CO: University of Colorado Institute of Behavioral Science.

Bakun, William H., and Allan G. Lindh. 1985. "The Parkfield, California, Earthquake Prediction Experiment." *Science* 229:619-624.

Baldwin, Tamara K. 1991. "Earthquake Awareness in Southeast Missouri: A Study in Pluralistic Ignorance." Paper presented at the Conference on Public and Media Response to Earthquake Forecasts, Southern Illinois University at Edwardsville, May 16-18. Cape Girardeau, MO: Southeast Missouri State University, Department of Mass Communication.

Bay Area Earthquake Preparedness Project. 1989. "The Complexities of Earthquake Prediction." *Networks* 4(1):6-8.

Blalock Jr., Hubert M., and Ann B. Blalock. 1968. *Methodology in Social Research.* New York: McGraw-Hill.

Bolt, Bruce A. 1978. *Earthquakes: A Primer*. San Francisco: W. H. Freeman.

Bolt, Bruce A., and Richard H. Jahns. 1979. "California's Earthquake Hazard: A Reassessment." *Public Affairs Report* 20(4):1-9.

California Seismic Safety Commission. 1991. *California at Risk: Reducing Earthquake Hazards 1992-1996*. Sacramento, CA: California Seismic Safety Commission.

Campbell, Donald T., and Julian C. Stanley. 1963. Experimental and Quasi-Experimental Designs for Research. Chicago: Rand-McNally.

Committee on Socioeconomic Effects of Earthquake Prediction. 1978. *A Program of Studies on the Socioeconomic Effects of Earthquake Prediction*. National Research Council. Washington, DC: National Academy of Sciences.

Danzig, Elliott R., Paul W. Thayer, and Lila R. Galater. 1958. *The Effects of a Threatening Rumor on a Disaster-Stricken Community*. Disease Study #10. Disaster Research Group. Washington, DC: National Academy of Sciences.

Dillman, Donald A. 1978. *Mail and Telephone Surveys: The Total Design Method*. New York: Wiley.

Earthquake Engineering Research Institute. 1989. "Social Impact and Emergency Response." Pp. 150-160 in *Earthquake Spectra* (Special Supplement). Oakland, CA: Earthquake Engineering Research Institute.

Echevarria, Julio A., Kathryn A. Norton, and Roger D. Norton. 1986. "The Socioeconomic Consequences of Earthquake Prediction." *Earthquake Prediction Research* 4:175-193.

Edwards, Margie L. 1991. "Public Response to the Browning Prediction: Some Preliminary Findings." Paper presented at the Conference on Public and Media Response to Earthquake Forecasts, Southern Illinois University at Edwardsville, May 16-18. Newark, DE: University of Delaware, Disaster Research Center.

Executive Office of the President. 1978. *The National Earthquake Hazards Reduction Program*. Washington, DC

Farley, John E., Hugh D. Barlow, Marvin S. Finkelstein, Larry Riley, and Lewis G. Bender. 1991. "Earthquake Hysteria, Before and After: A Survey and Follow-Up on Public Response to the Browning Forecast." Paper presented at the Conference on Public and Media Response to Earthquake Forecasts, Southern Illinois University at Edwardsville, May 16-18. Edwardsville, IL: Southern Illinois University, Department of Sociology.

Federal Emergency Management Agency. 1985. *An Action Plan for Reducing Earthquake Hazards of Existing Buildings*. Washington, DC: The Federal Emergency Management Agency Earthquake Programs.

_____. 1987. *National Earthquake Hazards Reduction Program: Fiscal Year 1987 Activities*. Report to the United States Congress. Washington, DC: Federal Emergency Management Agency.

Fitzpatrick, Colleen, and Paul W. O'Brien. 1992. "Social Response to the First "A" Alert of the Parkfield Earthquake Prediction Experiment." Report QR54 to the Natural Hazards Research and Applications Information Center. Boulder, CO: University of Colorado.

Fitzpatrick, Colleen, and Dennis S. Mileti. 1990. "Perception and Response to Aftershock Warnings During the Emergency Period." Pp. 75-83 in *The Loma Prieta Earthquake: Studies of Short-Term Impacts*, edited by Robert Bolin. Boulder, CO: University of Colorado Institute of Behavioral Science.

Fogleman, Charles W. 1958. *Family and Community in Disaster: A Socio-Psychological Study of the Effects of a Major Disaster upon Individuals and Groups*. Unpublished Ph.D. Dissertation. Baton Rouge, LA: Louisiana State University.

Governor's Board of Inquiry. 1990. *Competing Against Time*. North Highlands, CA: State of California, Office of Planning and Research.

Haas, J. Eugene and Dennis S. Mileti. 1976. *Social Effects of Earthquake Prediction*. Boulder, CO: University of Colorado Institute of Behavioral Science.

Hamilton, Robert M. 1976. "The Status of Earthquake Prediction." Pp. 6-9 in *Earthquake Prediction—Opportunity to Avert Disaster*. Arlington, VA: U.S. Geological Survey.

Harris, Stephen L. 1990. *Agents of Chaos: Earthquakes, Volcanoes, and Other Natural Disasters*. Missoula, MT: Mountain Press.

Heppenheimer, T.A. 1988. *The Coming Quake*. New York: Times Books.

Hirose, Hirotada. 1985. "Earthquake Prediction in Japan and the United States." *International Journal of Mass Emergencies and Disasters* 3(1):51-66.

House Committee on Banking, Finance and Urban Affairs. 1990. *Earthquake Hazard Mitigation and Earthquake Insurance: Hearings Before the Subcommittee on Policy Research and Insurance of the Committee on Banking, Finance and Urban Affairs House of Representatives*. Washington, DC: U.S. Government Printing Office.

Iversen, Gudmund R. 1979. *Statistics for Sociology*. Dubuque, IA: Wm. C. Brown.

Joint Committee on Seismic Safety. 1974. *Meeting the Earthquake Challenge*. Sacramento, CA: California Division of Mines & Geology.

Kates, Robert W., and David Pijawka. 1977. "From Rubble to Monument: The Pace of Reconstruction." Pp. 1-4 in *Reconstruction Following Disaster*, edited by J. Eugene Haas, Robert W. Kates, and Martyn J. Bowden. Cambridge, MA: MIT Press.

Kennedy, John M. 1991. "Hoosier Reactions to the Predictions of an Earthquake." Paper presented at the Conference on Public and Media Response to Earthquake Forecasts, Southern Illinois University at Edwardsville, May 16-18. Indiana University, Center for Survey Research.

Klockars, Alan J., and Gilbert Sax. 1986. *Multiple Comparisons*. SAGE Publications Series on Quantitative Applications in the Social Sciences. Beverly Hills, CA: Sage.

Kunreuther, Howard, with Ralph Ginsberg, Louis Miller, Philip Sagi, Paul Slovic, Bradley Borkan, and Norman Katz. 1978. *Disaster Insurance Protection Public Policy Lessons*. New York: John Wiley.

Leonard II, Wilbert Marcellus. 1976. *Basic Social Statistics*. San Francisco: West.

Lewis-Beck, Michael S. 1980. *Applied Regression: An Introduction*. SAGE Publications Series on Quantitative Applications in the Social Sciences. Newbury Park, CA: Sage.

Lindh, Allan G. 1990. "Earthquake Prediction Comes of Age." *Technology Review* February/March:42-51.

Mader, George G. 1980. "Seismic Hazard Mitigation Through Land Use Planning." Pp. 176-179 in *Proceedings of Conference XII: Earthquake Prediction Information*, edited by Walter W. Hays. Menlo Park, CA: U.S. Geological Survey.

Mader, George G., William E. Spangle, and Martha L. Blair. 1980. *Land Use Planning After Earthquakes*. Portola Valley, CA: William Spangle and Associates.

Mann, Arthur E. 1979. *The Field Act and California Schools*. Sacramento, CA: State of California Seismic Safety Commission.

Mileti, Dennis S. 1982. "Public Perceptions of Seismic Hazards and Critical Facilities." *Bulletin of the Seismological Society of America* 72(6):S13-S18.

Mileti, Dennis S., and Janice R. Hutton. 1986. *Initial Response to the 5 April 1985 Parkfield Earthquake Prediction*. Boulder, CO: University of Colorado Natural Hazards Research Applications and Information Center.

Mileti, Dennis S., and Paul W. O'Brien. 1992. "Warnings During Disaster: Normalizing Communicated Risk." *Social Problems* 39(1):40-57.

Mileti, Dennis S., and John H. Sorensen. 1990. *Communication of Emergency Public Warnings: A Social Science Perspective and State-of-the-Art Assessment*. Washington, DC: Federal Emergency Management Agency.

Mileti, Dennis S., Janice R. Hutton, and John H. Sorensen. 1981. *Earthquake Prediction Response and Options for Public Policy.* Boulder, CO: University of Colorado Institute of Behavioral Science.

Miller, Russell. 1983. *Continents in Collision.* Alexandria, VA: Time-Life Books.

National Academy of Engineering. 1969. *Earthquake Engineering Research.* Washington, DC: National Academy of Sciences.

National Research Council. 1969a. *Seismology: Responsibilities and Requirements of a Growing Science.* Washington, DC: National Academy of Sciences.

_____. 1969b. *Toward Reduction of Losses from Earthquakes: Conclusions from the Great Alaska Earthquake of 1964.* Washington, DC: National Academy of Sciences.

Obermeier, Stephen F. 1986. "Earthquake-Induced Sand Blows near Charleston, South Carolina." Washington, DC: Department of the Interior, U.S. Geological Survey.

Office of Emergency Preparedness. 1972. *Report to the Congress: Disaster Preparedness.* Washington, DC: Executive Office of the President.

Olson, Richard S., Bruno Podesta, and Joanne M. Nigg. 1989. *The Politics of Earthquake Prediction.* Princeton, NJ: Princeton University Press.

Olson, Robert A., Constance Holland, H. Grana Miller, W. Henry Lambright, Henry J. Lagorio, and Carl R. Treseder. 1988. *To Save Lives and Protect Property: A Policy Assessment of Federal Earthquake Activities, 1964-1987.* Sacramento, CA: VSP Associates.

Palm, Risa. 1981. *Real Estate Agents and Special Studies Zones Disclosure: The Response of California Home Buyers to Earthquake Hazards Information.* Boulder, CO: University of Colorado Institute of Behavioral Science.

_____. 1990. *Natural Hazards: An Integrative Framework for Research and Planning.* Baltimore, MD: Johns Hopkins University Press.

Perry, Ronald W. and Marjorie R. Greene. 1982. *Citizen Response to Volcanic Eruptions: The Case of Mount St. Helens.* New York: Irvington.

Roberts, R. Blaine, Jerome W. Milliman, and Richard W. Ellson. 1982. *Earthquakes and Earthquake Prediction: Simulating Their Economic Effects.* Columbia, SC: University of South Carolina College of Business Administration.

Shipman Jr., Jöhn M., Gilbert L. Fowler, and Russell E. Shain. 1991. "Iben Browning and the Fault: Newspaper Coverage of an Earthquake Prediction." Paper presented at the Conference on Public and Media Response to Earthquake Forecasts, Southern Illinois University at Edwardsville, May 16-18. State University, AR: Arkansas State University, College of Communications.

Southern California Earthquake Preparedness Project. 1985. *The Parkfield and San Diego Earthquake Predictions: A Chronology*. Los Angeles: Governor's Office of Emergency Preparedness.

Spangle and Associates. 1991. *Rebuilding After Earthquakes: Lessons for Planners*. Portola Valley, CA: William Spangle and Associates.

Stallings, Robert A. 1982. "Social Aspects Related to the Dissemination and Credibility of Earthquake Predictions in Cross-Cultural Perspective." Pp. 59-67 in *Proceedings of Earthquake Prediction*. Tokyo, Japan: Terra Scientific and UNESCO.

Stevenson, D.A., P. Talwani, and D.C. Amick. 1976. "Recent Seismic Activity near Lake Jocassee, Oconee Co., South Carolina: Preliminary Results and a Successful Earthquake Prediction." *EOS* 57:290. Washington, DC: American Geophysical Union.

Stolz, C., L.R. Sykes, and Y.P. Aggarwal. 1973. "Earthquake Predictions: A Physical Basis." *Science* 181:803-810.

Sylvester, Judith. 1991. "Media Research Bureau/Suburban Journals Earthquake Prediction Poll." Paper presented at the Conference on Public and Media Response to Earthquake Forecasts, Southern Illinois University at Edwardsville, May 16-18. Columbia, MO: University of Missouri, School of Journalism.

Tobin, L. Thomas, Fred Turner, James F. Goodfellow and Brian L. Stoner. 1992. "California at Risk: Where do We Go from Here?" *Earthquake Spectra* 8(1):17-34.

Turner, Ralph H. 1983. "Waiting for Disaster: Changing Reactions to Earthquake Forecasts in Southern California." *International Journal of Mass Emergencies and Disasters* 1:307-334.

Turner, Ralph H., Joanne M. Nigg, and Denise H. Paz. 1986. *Waiting for Disaster: Earthquake Watch in California*. Los Angeles, CA: University of California Press.

Turner, Ralph H., Joanne M. Nigg, Denise H. Paz, and Barbara S. Young. 1978. *Community Response to Earthquake Threat in Southern California: I. Individual Awareness and Attitudes*. Los Angeles, CA: University of California at Los Angeles Institute for Social Science Research.

_____. 1984. *Waiting for Disaster*. Berkeley, CA: University of California Press.

U.S. Bureau of the Census. 1982. "Characteristics of the Populations." *1980 Census of Population.* U.S. Government Printing Office. Washington, DC: Department of Commerce.

_____. 1983. *1980 Census of Population.* Chapter C, General Social and Economic Characteristics, Part 6, Section 4, Table 167. Washington, DC: Department of Commerce.

U.S. Geological Survey. 1966. *The Alaska Earthquake: March 27, 1964, Investigations and Reconstruction.* Washington, DC: Department of the Interior.

_____. 1976. *Earthquake Prediction and Hazard Mitigation: Options for USGS and NSF Programs.* Washington, DC: Department of the Interior.

_____. 1989a. *The Loma Prieta, California Earthquake of October 17th.* Reston, VA: U.S. Geological Survey.

_____. 1989b. *Loma Prieta Seismicity Update 5pm PDT 18 October.* Menlo Park, CA: U.S. Geological Survey.

_____. 1989c. *Loma Prieta Seismicity Press Release: 10am PDT 21 October.* Menlo Park, CA: U.S. Geological Survey.

_____. 1989d. *Aftershock Sequence Observations and Forecast: Monday October 23, 7am PDT.* Menlo Park, CA: U.S. Geological Survey.

_____. 1990. "Probabilities of Large Earthquakes in the San Francisco Bay Region, California. Washington, DC: Department of the Interior.

U.S. Geological Survey Staff. 1990. "The Loma Prieta, California, Earthquake: An Anticipated Event." *Science* 247:286-293.

Walker, Bryce. 1982. *Earthquake.* Alexandria, VA: Time-Life Books.

Wallace, Robert E., James F. Davis, and Karen C. McNally. 1984. "Terms for Expressing Earthquake Potential, Prediction, and Probability." *Bulletin of the Seismological Society of America* 74(5):1819-1825.

Webb, Eugene J., Donald T. Campbell, Richard D. Schwartz, and Lee Sechrest. 1966. *Unobtrusive Measures: Nonreactive Research in the Social Sciences.* Chicago: Rand McNally.

Weisbecker, Leo W., Ward C. Stoneman, and Staff. 1977. *Earthquake Prediction, Uncertainty, and Policies for the Future.* Menlo Park, CA: Stanford Research Institute.

Wesson, Robert L., and Robert E. Wallace. 1985. "Predicting the Next Great Earthquake in California." *Scientific American* 252(2):35-43.

White, Gilbert F., and J. Eugene Haas. 1975. *Assessment of Research on Natural Hazards.* Cambridge, MA: MIT Press.

Working Group on California Earthquake Probabilities. 1988. *Probabilities of Large Earthquakes Occurring in California on the San Andreas Fault.* Washington, DC: Department of the Interior, U.S. Geological Survey.

Working Group on Earthquake Hazards Reduction. 1978. *Earthquake Hazards Reduction: Issues for an Implementation Plan.* Washington, DC: Executive Office of the President.

Yong, Chen. 1988. "Earthquake Prediction Countermeasures in China." Paper presented at the Plenary Session of the International Symposium of Earthquake Countermeasures, Beijing, China, May 10-13.

Zeigler, Donald J., and James M. Johnson, Jr. 1984. "Evacuation Behavior in Response to Nuclear Power Plant Accident." *Professional Geographer* 36:207-215.

About the Authors

Dennis S. Mileti is a professor of sociology and the director of the Hazards Assessment Laboratory at Colorado State University. He received his Ph.D. in sociology from the University of Colorado, Boulder, in 1974, and his M.A. and B.A. degrees in sociology were awarded in 1971 and 1968, respectively, from California State University at Los Angeles and the University of California at Los Angeles.

Professor Mileti is the author of over 100 publications, most of which focus on societal aspects of emergency preparedness and natural and technological hazards mitigation. He has served as chairperson of the Committee on Natural Disasters in the National Research Council of the National Academy of Sciences and as a member of the Advisory Board on Research to the U.S. Geological Survey. He has a variety of practical experiences related to hazards mitigation and preparedness, including serving as a consultant to utilities to develop emergency response plans for nuclear power plants, and he has been a staff member of the California Seismic Safety Commission.

His current research is on corporate, government, and public response to revised earthquake probabilities following the Loma Prieta earthquake in the San Francisco Bay Area. He is also currently coordinating a national effort to assess research and applications knowledge and needs regarding natural hazards in the United States.

Colleen Fitzpatrick is a research scientist with the Hazards Assessment Laboratory at Colorado State University. She received her Ph.D. in sociology from Colorado State University in 1992. Her M.A. and B.A. degrees in sociology were earned in 1985 and 1979, respectively, from California State University at Northridge. She is the author of several papers and journal articles on the sociological aspects of risk communication.

Dr. Fitzpatrick joined the research staff of the Hazards Assessment Laboratory in 1987. She has served as a research sociologist on National Science Foundation grants for studying organizational response to weather modification, earthquake risk communication involving the Parkfield earthquake prediction experiment, public aftershock warnings during the Loma Prieta earthquake emergency, public response to revised earthquake probabilities in the San Francisco Bay Area, and social response to the first short-term prediction of the Parkfield experiment.

Index